Sunshine

THROUGH THE

Rain

A Bouquet of Inspirational Thoughts

RITA JANTZEN HOCHSTETLER

2673 TR 421
Sugarcreek, OH 44681

Carlisle Printing
WALNUT CREEK

Dedication

To my husband, John, and our children, Shane, Lance, and Heather, who share in the ministry of suffering with me. This is also dedicated to those who walk hand in hand with suffering and to children of all ages.

Contents

Acknowledgments

Many thanks to Aneta Good for her poetry. It has completed this book. Aneta shares in the ministry of suffering, because of the loss of her husband.

I also give my thanks to Lavonne, Mrs. Lowell Koehn, for proofreading and correcting my writings. I appreciate her service. She knows suffering in the loss of their son.

Introduction

As I learned to lean on my walking aids, God taught me to lean harder on Him. In yielding to my wheelchair and the care of loved ones, I need to abandon my wishes and will to Him. I have written of the life I know. When I started writing, I was able to sit on a common household chair by my desk, now I sit in my wheelchair. Then I could type with both hands, now I type with only one hand.

This book speaks of the desire of my heart for myself and all suffering humanity. May we all learn to lean harder on Him who loves us.

Rita Jantzen Hochstetler

The Ministry of
Suffering

An Allegory on Suffering

Suffering is referred to in the female gender, because it can multiply. Different types of suffering are mental, emotional, of which false accusations are a part of, physical, financial, the loss of a loved one, and spiritual loss, or a loved one going astray.

I was walking along life's pathway when the Lord spoke to me so quietly that I had to bend a little nearer to hear Him. "I will send a companion especially for you, to help you make it to yonder city," He said.

Before long I felt rather than saw a presence walking beside me. The path really did not seem that rugged, but then I stubbed my toe. As my companion reached out to steady me, I felt a slight sensation. Not understanding from where it came, I ignored it.

Soon I stumbled again. Again this presence reached out to give me a helping hand. Why did I receive a shock when help was what I needed? I turned to take a look and did not comprehend who my companion was.

After a fall, my companion again reached for me, and this time I recognized who she was. She with a sad face was Suffering. I cried in terror, "Jesus." He was instantly by my side, drew me close to Himself, and said, "Peace, be still."

"But, Lord," I cried, "why must I walk hand in hand with Suffering?"

"Hush, My child," He replied as He took my hand in His. Then I felt the scar in His hand and knew He had suffered and died for me. I became willing to suffer with Him.

After a time, I felt a stab of pain in my side and knew who my constant companion was. Again I cried, "Jesus, why?"

He was by my side and whispered, "Lo, I am with you always." He did not need to give me an answer; He did not owe me one. I had His promise, and that was sufficient. Then I understood that He is ever with me even when Suffering is my companion. I could not help but have a song of thanksgiving. I learned to love my Savior more.

In time, I learned that if I would sing a song of praise, Suffering's touch did not sting as much. So when I needed a helping hand, I did not shrink so from her touch. I was on my way to yonder celestial city to be face to face with my Redeemer. The nearer I got to home, the more I could feel Suffering's touch. I also became more and more aware of my suffering Savior. I loved Him more. With joy and anticipation, I looked forward to home.

Then one day Jesus was by my side, and taking my other hand in His, He took me to the bank of the Jordan River. He again whispered, "Fear none of those things which thou shalt suffer...be thou faithful unto death, and I will give thee a crown of life" (Rev. 2:10). He then led me through the swelling current and, releasing my hand from Suffering's hand, said, "Welcome home!" Then He placed my hand in the hand of Glory's, saying, "This is your new companion now."

Oh, joy forever and ever!

Pearls because of Suffering

One day a mother and her young son and daughter were walking along a beach digging for clams. As they were digging, they were discussing other marine and sea life. They talked of seafoods that they especially liked to eat—clams, shrimp, lobster, and oysters.

"Speaking of oysters," Mother said, "did you know that sometimes an oyster will get a particle of sand between its body and shell that causes it much discomfort?"

The young girl, having a gentle and caring disposition, asked, "But, Mommy, what happens to the oyster then? I know he can't open his shell and take it out."

"You're right, he can't," said Mother. Then she went on to explain, "God has wondrously provided a means for the oyster to produce a substance that coats the particle causing the irritation. That way it becomes bearable to the oyster, and he can adapt to his problem. But if the oyster were to fight against the irritant, then it would cause an infection or a disease."

Mother continued, "It is the same in our lives. When a disappointment or sorrow befalls us, then the love of Jesus and knowing what He suffered for us should be the 'substance' that coats our suffering. But if we, like an oyster, cannot adapt to what we are called to bear, it could become an 'infection' or a bitterness to us, eventually causing us spiritual death."

Then Mother told them that when the oyster dies and his shell is opened, a pearl is found where the irritation had been.

We can take a lesson from this, knowing that whatever we may be called to suffer, if we allow Jesus to "coat" it with His love, we can bear it. A "pearl," a grace, a beautiful spirit, will form and be found in us.

Thanks and Praise

"O give thanks unto the Lord, for he is good: for his mercy endureth forever" (Ps. 107:1, also 1 Chron. 16:34).

"O give thanks unto the Lord, for he is good." Note, it doesn't say to give thanks when things are going good or "my way"; it just says "to give thanks."

Giving thanks and praise go hand in hand. There are two songs to be sung in life. One is the song of praise and should be sung whatever life may bring—even during a trial. The other is the song of deliverance.

I think the most important is the song of praise during a trial. Praising God without seeing Him or even feeling His presence is a mark of our confidence and faith in Him. Knowing that He is fighting our battles and that He will be the winner is praiseworthy!

In pondering Naaman and his leprosy, we will recall how angry he was when he was told to wash in the Jordan River. At first, he refused, but later he repented and went. Let us look at this experience, thinking of ourselves.

When Naaman stepped into the water, he could have been disgusted and thought, "Why do I need to go through this? Why me? This is more than I can bear, this dirty, smelly river. Life isn't fair."

Taking one dip and looking at his arms, he sees he still has leprosy. The feelings of resentment and agitation stir in his heart. But he takes another dip, and another. Are we not the same, often needing more than one dip for a healing or for learning?

Finally, he does submit. Taking the last dip, he looks and sees he is healed!

Can we imagine the thankfulness for the Jordan River that wells up in his heart? Dashing from the river, his heart was, no doubt, swelling with praises.

When we reach the other side, we will say, "Thank You for walking with me through the valleys, rivers, and hills, the shadows and sunshine, the tears and joyful times. Thank You for turning me from my willful way. O Father, thank You!"

Diamonds in the Rough

When we are called to the ministry of suffering, we need a reassurance of God's love. A verse to draw courage from is, "For I reckon that the sufferings of this present time are not worthy to be compared with the glory which shall be revealed in us" (Rom. 8:18).

We are as diamonds in the rough, and God uses stinging blows to chisel and mold us to fit us for His crown. Someday we will bring honor and glory to God if we are faithful to Him. We need to remind ourselves of this when called to bear the burden of suffering. Surely not a blow will fall upon us but what the love of God has permitted it.

Some may think that these things are happenstance and that we need to allow God to work in us. That may be, but all may not be cruel chance. "...the Lord hath his way in the whirlwind and in the storm..." (Nahum 1:3). Surely we are kept in the hollow of His hand.

Here is a thought to ponder, "The chamber of suffering—is it not the birthplace of obedience?"

Even though suffering is my companion now, someday when I come to the Jordan River, I will exchange this my companion for a new one, and this one will be Glory. So you see, God allows suffering to prepare us for Heaven and to meet Him who created us.

God is very good to us, and we do not deserve His goodness. When one reads Exodus 4:11, "...or who maketh the dumb, or deaf, or the seeing, or the blind? Have not I the Lord?" then we can see God has a plan for our lives.

Another verse we read says, "I form the light, and create darkness: I bring peace [prosperity] and create evil [disaster]; I the Lord do all these things" (Isa. 45:7). He rules and is master over all. Nothing happens without Him allowing it. We need to trust Him, for He has a loving hand over us. "For I know the thoughts that I think toward you, saith the Lord, thoughts of peace and not of evil..." (Jer. 29:11).

Taking Another Look

Betty had a debilitating disease. She prayed often that God's grace and love would sustain her, that she would be able to accept what had come to her.

Then one day her husband had a visitor. The visitor said Betty had sin in her life, hence the disease. Though Betty's husband tried to shield her from this, Betty learned of their visitor's opinion. At first Betty was shocked that anyone could have the idea that a disease denoted a person had an unconfessed sin in his life. The next reaction was anger; after all, she had had this disease since childhood. After a time, she thought, "But it won't hurt me to take another look at myself." She bowed her head and said, "Lord, help me to take another look. I want to make sure I am Your child."

That night before retiring, she searched her life and heart; she asked the Lord to forgive her where she had sinned. She asked Jesus again to live with her.

She slept and had this dream. She dreamed she was standing by a pond, and Jesus came to her. He pointed out a sign that said, "No fishing." Then He said, "I have forgiven all; don't go back and fish for things that have been forgiven." Her dream faded, and she awoke. Joy flooded her heart.

Betty was so happy, and she awoke her husband to tell him. She told him she was thankful that the visitor had come to their house. She was also thankful the visitor said she had sin in her life, because this is what caused her to look deep inside. Her dream was precious, and she could only have it because she was called to a search.

Stars in the Night

It is a beautiful sight to go outside on a clear, dark night and look up into the sky and see the stars. The blacker the sky, the more brilliant the star-studded sky looks. The stars look like diamonds glittering and twinkling on black velvet. The same stars are in the sky when the sun is blazing, but they cannot be seen for the brightness of the sun.

Let us compare our life to the stars. We are like a star, and in order to show the brilliance of our star for God, or to bring Him honor and glory, we may be called to a life of suffering, which compares to the black sky.

If we live a life of ease, which is compared to a bright, sunny day, our star of love for God will not show up as clearly.

Another comparison is a diamond against a dark cloth. Have you ever wondered why the diamonds in a jewelry store are displayed against a black cloth? That is so they will show up more brilliantly.

So also when our life is against the black cloth of suffering and we are faithful, then we shine more brilliantly for God's honor and glory.

Our Work

First Timothy 2:1 reads, "Exhort therefore, that, first of all, supplications, prayers, intercessions, and giving of thanks be made for all men." In simple English, "This is my advice, make humble entreaties, praying much for others, pleading for God to give them direction and mercy; giving thanks for all he has done and will do for them."

There is much work to be done. There are many prayers to be prayed, so many people to be prayed for.

Whatever one's condition, whether bedfast, in a wheelchair, shy or bashful, one can pray for someone, pleading for God to give conviction, bestowing His mercy and goodness on them. We need to remember the prayer of thanksgiving, thanking God for answered prayers for our loved ones, but how many of us remember to thank God for all He will do?

There is work for everyone.

Faith

God has healing for mankind, spiritually, physically, mentally, and emotionally. Sometimes, though, God does not choose to heal us physically as He has other plans for us. His will is for us always to be healed spiritually. Spiritual healing brings emotional and mental healing.

A requirement for healing is faith in God, not faith in faith. A preparation for healing is reading about it in the Bible.

These verses are faith builders: Proverbs 4:20-22; Romans 10:17; Matthew 4:23-24; 7:7,11; 14:14; 8:7,13,17; 9:29,35; 15:30; 17:20-21; 19:2; Mark 1:34; 5:34; 10:52; 9:23; 11:22-24; Luke 6:19; John 10:10; 14:13-14; Acts 10:28; Galatians 3:13; 3 John 2; Hebrews 13:8; Malachi 4:2; Psalms 6:2; 30:2; 41:4; 42:11; 91:9,10; 103:2,3; Proverbs 3:7,8; Exodus 15:26; James 5:15; 1 Peter 2:24; Isaiah 53: 4,5; Jeremiah 17:14; and 1 John 4:4.

With so great a God to go to, we should have no fears or wants, nor should we faint. We can go to God's treasure-house and take whatever we have need of. If we feel faint and have need of more courage, let's pray, asking God to give. Then let us pick it up and go on. Also, remember, you may find it in the Bible, that storehouse of rich treasures.

God can supply you with all. Learn the skill of asking Him. Go to Him often in prayer; this is our greatest privilege.

More Like Thee

The summer vacation Bible school children were singing, "He's still working on me, To make me what I ought to be." The melody and words kept going over in Lucy's mind. She was the kindergarten teacher, and, yes, God was still working on her. She bowed her head and prayed, "Don't give up on me, Lord. I want to be saved. I want to become more like You."

Several years later Lucy was in a doctor's office and learned she had a lifelong illness. It was not an easy matter to accept. Then one day as she was having devotions, she remembered her prayer of several years before when she asked Jesus to make her more like Him. Is this what it was going to take? "Father," she cried, "this is more than I can bear. The cup is too bitter for me to drink."

Instantly He was by her side and said, "Peace, be still. I have walked the way before you, suffered every pain and woe. I'll not leave you but will be with you each step of the way."

Then He added, "You will see me in your loved ones when they give you a helping hand. Your spiritual brothers and sisters will mention your name in prayer and also give aid where needed."

Lucy bowed her head and prayed, "Have Thine own way, Lord. Thou art the Potter, I am the clay." Lucy learned to be thankful, to praise the Lord, but best of all, she learned to love Him more. Those times when the way seems dark and dreary, Lucy still hears the comforting Voice say, "Peace, be still."

God's Plan

Often Sara would read, "For I know the thoughts that I think toward you, saith the Lord, thoughts of peace, and not of evil, to give you an expected end" (Jer. 29:11). Sara always felt comforted when she read that verse; after all, it was a promise from God.

Then one day as she and her husband, Dave, were out for their daily walk, he said, "Sara, you have stumbled several times today. Is something wrong?"

"No, I think it is just my shoes," she answered.

A day or so later on their walk, Dave spoke again, "Sara, I notice that you are limping. Do you have pain?"

"Oh, no, everything is fine. I don't think I'm limping."

"But you are, dear. Do you think something could be wrong?"

"Well, no, nothing is wrong. After all, this morning I read a special promise from God that He has thoughts of peace and not evil towards me."

About a month later, Dave's parents came to visit. When Dave and Sara were ready for their daily walk, they invited his parents to walk with them. As they were walking, Dave's mother said, "Sara, you are limping. Is something wrong?" Sara again remembered the verse she had read a month earlier.

Several months later Dave said, "Sara, we need to find out what is wrong. You limp and stumble a lot." They went to a doctor who told them Sara had an incurable illness.

Often Sara would go to the Bible for comfort, and sometimes she would read Jeremiah 29:11. What did it mean? It seemed like an evil calamity had befallen her. Then one day as Sara awoke from her nap, she heard the still small voice say, "I know the thoughts that I think towards you, thoughts of peace, and not of evil, to give you an expected end."

Then it opened up to her that God had only her good in mind. He was preparing her to walk on gold. It was not evil—He longed for her to share in His splendor. She bowed her head and said, "Lord, thank You for choosing me. I am glad I am Yours and You are mine."

A Heart of Thanksgiving

Good morning! What a lovely morning! The sun is smiling on the world while the sky is lovely and blue. I can hear the birds and the wind chimes in the soft gentle breeze. Life is truly good.

As my thoughts begin to wander, I remember a morning when, twenty-three years ago, I opened my eyes and saw daylight but not much more. I recall the doctor saying my sight might never return, or it if did, I could awake any morning blind again.

So it is that with a heart bubbling over with thankfulness, I thank the Lord I can see. Hearing the birds, I whisper a thanksgiving that I can hear. My daughter comes into my room. "Mom," she asks, "are you ready to get up?" Soon the telephone rings.

"Hello, how are you today?" After a nice visit, my friend says, "I just wanted you to know I have been thinking of you and pray for you."

Thank You, Lord, for love of family and friends. Thank You for grace and salvation which gives me a home in Heaven. Forgive me for those times when I complain and am not willing to bear my ministry of suffering. Thank · You for Your love.

Tears in a Bottle

Psalm 56:8: "Thou tellest my wanderings: put thou my tears into thy bottle: are they not in thy book?"

Revelation 5:8: "And when he had taken the book, the four beasts and four and twenty elders fell down before the Lamb, having every one of them harps, and golden vials full of odours, which are the prayers of saints."

The most perfect prayers are those that have been anointed with tears. When praying for ourselves or wayward loved ones, or those who we know are in turmoil and struggles, and the prayers are bathed in tears, the Bible says it releases a beautiful odor to the Lord.

"Are they not in thy book?" When a teardrop drops on a celestial page, God causes a beautiful writing to appear in His book that reveals the contents of our hearts. Let us not be ashamed to have our eyes washed with tears.

Other times we have tears of sorrow and disappointments, possibly because of the loss of a loved one to a disease, or possibly a parent finds out he has a disabling disease and will not be able to work. Or it could be someone has an accident and will never walk again. Parents may wait anxiously for a child to be born, only to discover their child has a birth defect and will require extra care and attention. A loved one is taken in a tragic accident, causing tears of anguish.

We have a song that says God sees our tears and hears them when they fall. He cares; tears are a language He understands.

We know that when we enter Heaven, God Himself will wipe the tears from our eyes. But these tears that have been kept in bottles, I believe, will be changed to diamonds.

Suffering and Compassion

"And the Lord said unto him, Who hath made man's mouth? or who maketh the dumb, or deaf, or the seeing, or the blind? have not I the Lord?" (Exod. 4:11).

"But though he cause grief, yet will he have compassion according to the multitude of his mercies. For he doth not afflict willingly nor grieve the children of men" (Lam. 3:32,33).

When called to a ministry of suffering, we should not be so concerned with "why me" or the reason for the suffering. For the Bible says, "Blessed is the man whom thou chastenest, O Lord, and teachest him out of thy law (Ps. 94:12). His promises are all sufficient. "But my God shall supply all your need according to his riches in glory by Christ Jesus" (Phil.4:19). We need to remember His compassion, as stated in Lamentations, and become centered on God. Our God reigns! "The Lord reigneth..." (Ps. 93:1).

When we become centered on God, we come to know Him and His love. Then we can understand His compassion and pity towards us. "Like as a father pitieth his children, so the Lord pitieth them that fear him" (Ps. 103:13).

Now I can truly say, "But the Lord is my defence; and my God is the rock of my refuge" (Ps. 94:22).

Joy and Pleasure

"Thou wilt shew me the path of life: in thy presence is fulness of joy; at thy right hand there are pleasures for evermore" (Ps. 16:11).

The life lived for Christ is truly a blessed life. He has joy and pleasures, "surprise packages," planned for us all along the way. My surprises and joys are many. I would like to tell you about them.

I have much joy when I arise early and see the sunrise. The delight is real when a friend comes over with her happy smiling baby and energetic two-year-old son. To see their energy and hear their inquisitive questions about the world brings me joy. The times the school children call to say they would like to sing to me can bring tears of happiness. The young married couple who invites us to enjoy the fellowship of their home, or the busy mother who calls to say, "I have sewed a dress for you. May I bring it over?" Then there have been those who have called to say, "I canned three dozen quarts of green beans for you."

The young people who got money together to give a new wheelchair for Christmas, or the young married sisters who, instead of exchanging Christmas gifts, gave the money for a new pair of glasses. I cannot forget the many flowers and plants that have been given for my joy.

Then there is the time when our son said, "Mom, you need to see the beautiful day. I'll take you for a walk before I go to work."

Or the phone calls from relatives and friends just to say, "Hi, how are you? I'm thinking and praying for you." The gifts of some special household appliances and the loving care of my husband and daughter always bring thankfulness to my heart. The friends who are brave enough to handle a wheelchair to take me shopping or to go out for lunch are special.

I do not forget the neighbors who drop whatever they are busy with to give a helping hand when I have fallen or had a calamity. Also there are many who have brought a dish or meal over. Then there was the friend who gave me her old computer and printer. Because of them, I have discovered an interest in "writing."

The Spirit has had many pleasures and joys for me. To have His peace in my heart is the biggest joy of all. Thank You, Father, for Your love.

Complaints and Acceptance

"O Jesus, how long do I need to endure this unrelenting, devastating disease? When I want to turn over in bed, I cannot do it by myself."

"Child, I know and understand. When the nails held Me to the cross, I could not change positions either. You have a loved one who can come to your aid and give you some relief. My friends turned their backs on Me, and one of My best friends denied Me, claiming he never knew Me."

"Forgive me, Lord," I cried.

"Lord, I long to get up and fix my bed, to clean my room, or, better yet, to clean the whole house."

"Daughter, I know and understand. I had no place of my own, not even a place to lay My head."

"O Jesus, forgive me," I pray.

"Today, Lord, I would like to sew a dress," I plead. "You see our daughter has need of a new one, but my hands do not cooperate, and they hurt so," I complain.

"Dear daughter, I understand," He said, and He continued, "I had only one set of clothing, and then at My crucifixion, even that was taken from Me."

"Forgive again, Lord," I cry.

"Jesus, I have a desire to do great things for my family today. I would like to cook, clean house, press and mend clothes for them, but here I am stuck to my wheelchair."

"Dear one, I know how it is. I longed to comfort and care for My mother, but I was nailed to a cross. So I asked My friend to care for her."

"I'm sorry, Jesus. I know You understand."

"Today, Lord, all I ask for is just to care for myself," I beg. "But it seems I cannot even do that. I always need to ask my loved ones for help."

"Dear daughter, I understand. When I was hanging on the cross and the flies buzzed around the wounds caused by the leather whip, I could not even chase them away."

"I am sorry I've complained, Lord. I do not want my way but Thine, Lord. Thank you for loving me. Thank you for dying for me."

"For we have not an high priest which cannot be touched with the feeling of our infirmities; but was in all points tempted like as we are, yet without sin" (Heb. 4:15). In other words, Jesus can sympathize with us in every way, because He has felt all emotions and all temptations. He understands, and this helps us to bear what comes our way.

I'm Gonna Hold On

Did you ever have a day when it seemed you were forsaken? It happened to me recently. I had had a bad fall, and, oh, how my neck hurt. But worse yet, it seemed I was forsaken by God. Did God really care? If He did, why did I have multiple sclerosis when I had enjoyed being a homemaker, enjoyed having company?

I know of one woman who does not enjoy any part of homemaking, not cooking or keeping an orderly home, nor being hospitable. Why not let someone like that sit in a wheelchair so she can be cared for? Or how about the one who cannot enjoy the little ones she is entrusted with? Why then did I have to give up my desires of homemaking when there were others who did not appreciate their God-given tasks?

With such thoughts, I was very vulnerable to the devil's onslaughts. He whispered, "God doesn't really love you. If He did, you would not have MS. If He loved you, He would heal you." Immediately I recognized these thoughts were from the evil one and that he was working overtime. I barely had the strength to whisper, "Jesus, I need You."

Our daughter, sensing my discouragement, said, "Mom, God is suffering with you. He suffered for you at Calvary, and He is suffering with you now." Saying she had something I should read, she brought me the song, "I'm Gonna Hold On." She said I should pay special attention to verse two, "There are times we call on Jesus when He seems so far away. In those times we may not feel Him, but He hears us when we pray. Jesus knows our ev'ry heartache, for He's felt the pain we feel. So we need to hold on, hold on. I'm gonna hold on when the storms of life are raging. Hold on when there's trouble all around me. There are times when Satan tempts me, many things are hard to bear, But I'm gonna hold on, hold on."

Not only had Jesus heard my cry, but He had picked me up. "...lo, I am with you alway, even unto the end of the world" (Matt. 28:20).

God's Attributes

"Oh, no," I thought as I slid to the floor, "here I am alone in the house with no way to get up." Thankfully, I had my "First Alert" on to call for help. So I squeezed the button and settled down as comfortably as I could on the floor. I would have anywhere from ten minutes to a half hour to wait for help.

I wondered what to do with my time. First, I sang my theme song, "One More Valley." Then I got the idea to go through the alphabet and, with each letter, find a word describing God. For instance, A for Almighty, B for Benevolence, C for Comforter, D for Delightful, and so on. Time passed rapidly, and before I knew it, my help arrived.

The next time I needed to call for help, I thought of some new words for each letter. Other things I learned to do was sing songs I had memorized, pray for friends, loved ones, and those needing salvation, think of my blessings, praise God, or repeat memory verses. There was no need to be "down" just because I was down on the floor.

"Finally, brethren, whatsoever things are true, whatsoever things are honest, whatsoever things are just, whatsoever things are pure, whatsoever things are lovely, whatsoever things are of good report; if there be any virtue, and if there be any praise, think of these things" (Phil. 4:8).

Use Me

I had this song going over and over in my mind, "Use me, O my gracious Saviour, Use me, Lord, as pleaseth Thee: Nothing done for Thee so lowly But is great enough for me. Use me, Use me..." Why did this song keep going over in my mind? After all, I could not go to the mission. I am wheelchair bound and quite handicapped.

One morning our daughter was making breakfast for out-of-state company when the song came unbidden to my mind again. I puzzled, "Why at such times does that song come to my mind? I can't even get up and dress myself; how can God use me?"

Then there was just an ordinary day when again the song was on my mind. How puzzling! Why we lived out in the country, and very seldom did I see others. Well, on Sunday I went to church, but I did not see how I could be of much service there. I could not drive to the grocery store; in fact, I seldom saw the grocery store, so how could I witness?

"Lord," I prayed, "if there is anything I can do, You will have to make it plain to me. I want to be faithful."

Then came the day we were moving. I awakened with the song, "Use Me," on my mind again. Oh, how could I be of service when there were others that would have to do my work, helping my family move? It took prayers to not show discontent with my lot. Again I prayed, "Lord, help me to bear my ministry of suffering graciously so others may see You in me. But, Lord, tell me, how can I be of service to You when the song comes to my mind, 'Use Me'?

"Ah, Lord, is that the answer, to bear the ministry of suffering graciously and patiently? I'll need You every hour, for I cannot walk alone."

Yesterday and Tomorrow

There are two days in the week I never need to worry about. They are yesterday, as it is already past and gone, and tomorrow (if I know I am saved), as it has not arrived yet and may never come. "Take therefore no thought for the morrow: for the morrow shall take thought for the things of itself" (Matt. 6:34).

The hurts of yesterday need not be nursed or rehearsed. So how should one handle them? By forgiving them, giving them to our Burden Bearer, and then by being busy with our hands and minds in service for the Lord.

Another cure is singing praises to God.

> Sometimes I feel lonely and blue;
> Sometimes my heart breaks in two.
> Sometimes the sun won't shine through;
> Lord, I'll still sing praises to You.
>
> When your love is tested and tried
> And friends have turned you aside,
> Your spirit hurts deep inside.
> Lord, I'll still sing praises to You.
>
> When loved ones are passing away
> And you cannot seem to pray,
> Your heart cries all night and day.
> Lord, I'll still sing praises to You.
>
> No matter how much it rains,
> No matter how great the pain,
> In health or sickness, pain, or death,
> Lord, I'll still sing praises to You.

River of Love *by John Hochstetler. Permission granted.*

A Cross and Grace

"O Lord, my cross is too heavy," sobbed Miriam. "I not only cannot care for my family but I need to have them care for me. It is more than I can bear."

"Child, I understand what a heavy cross is. Mine was so heavy going up the hill to Calvary that Simon carried it for Me." Then He added, "I know yours is heavy for you, but let Me help you carry it, for when you are weak then am I strong."

Another day Miriam prayed, "Lord, the path I tread has so many rocks and thorns that it causes me to stumble often."

"Dear one, I know how painful thorns are, for the soldiers plaited a crown of thorns and put it upon My head. When the thorns in your path are too sharp, I will pick you up and carry you," He said.

"This cup is too bitter to drink; how can I drink it? Will You remove it from me?" pleaded Miriam.

"My daughter, I asked My Father to remove My bitter cup from Me, too, but it was His will for Me to drink it," Jesus answered. "I drank of your bitter cup at Calvary. I know how bitter it is. Give it to Me, and I will pour the wine of My love into it to sweeten it.

"Miriam, before I was crucified, I prayed the Father to send you the Comforter to abide with you forever. I prayed for you that your faith would remain strong, for the Father Himself loves you." (See John 14:16; 16:26,27; 17:9,10.)

"Jesus, how I love You! You are so good to me, so patient and kind. I can trust my all to You for I know you have borne all my sorrows and suffered every pain and woe."

"Thou art my God, and I will praise thee: thou art my God, I will exalt thee" (Ps. 118:28).

Why?

When reading the Easter story, we read where Jesus asked, "My God, why hast thou forsaken me?" It was not sin that Jesus asked, "Why?" but He does understand our whys, and He loves in spite of them.

How many of us have asked why at some point in our lives? We ask why because we may feel abandonment, which was what Jesus felt, or we may ask because of anger, which is sin.

Possibly we all have asked why at certain times in our lives. I know I have, but then it seemed wrong to me if I was questioning God, because He does not need to explain anything to anyone. He is God and Lord of all. He has given us His promises and love. That, we need to learn, is everything, it is all in all, it is enough. When we ask why, God does not give answers, but He gives us Himself!

"For he hath not despised nor abhorred the affliction of the afflicted; neither hath he hid his face from him; but when he cried unto him, he heard" (Ps. 22:24).

Tumbleweeds and Complaints

I remember as a young girl going to western Kansas to visit my uncles and aunts. Sometimes we would see the prairie wind blowing tumbleweeds about, and always they would drop bits of debris as they blew hither and yon.

We can be as a tumbleweed, blown about with a disappointment or an affliction, dropping complaints or debris wherever we go. But let us look to our perfect pattern as He suffered at Calvary. He did not complain about what could not be remedied, but He did speak of one of His physical sufferings. He said, " I thirst" (John 19:28). And that could be changed.

How much better for our loved ones if, instead of complaining about what cannot be changed, we would state our needs briefly, only requesting the possible.

Again, looking to Jesus, we see He did not complain but spoke briefly of what could easily be remedied. Then He did not complain of what had been offered Him, rather it was accepted without rebuke.

No one likes to suffer, but it does come. Jesus shares our suffering with us, showing us how to bear it without complaint, how to bear it gracefully.

Endurance

Who of us has not been tempted to give up or to "throw in the towel"?

Sixteen-year-old Rhonda felt inferior to her peers. She was not as outgoing as her sister, Jessica, nor, in her opinion, as good a singer as her friend Monica. In fact, was there anything she excelled in? She doubted it. You might as well give up, whispered a voice to her.

Michael's car was a discouraging disaster. First, there was a fuel leak; then there was the crack in the gasket, causing water to leak into the oil. Would the old thing ever be fixed? It was easy to feel down about his car. After all, most of his friends had not had to buy older models, or if they did, they could replace them when the cars gave too much trouble.

Why, come to think of it, most of the guys had dads who could set them up. "What's the use to keep on struggling?" Michael thought. "After all, at this rate, it will be years till I can afford to get married."

"What does this life have for me?" questioned Tara. "All my friends are married, and it seems like the girls who are getting married now are such young ones. What will I do? I certainly don't fit in. I know, I think I will travel, taking a tour of England and whatever else hits my fancy. After all, I deserve something good in life."

"I've been awake most of the night with this sick child," thought Brenda. "How will I ever get my work done? The green beans need to be picked and processed. John was asking for his jeans to be mended. Amanda needs her dress finished, and I'm, oh, so tired. Is there ever a break from it all?"

"Brenda feels like her road is rocky," thought John. "What about all the rain we've had? Now the sun is finally shining, but I work two days in the field and the tractor breaks down, needing a major overhaul. What could be rougher?"

"I am so tired of sitting in my wheelchair. And nursing homes? Well, for what they are, this one is as good or better than most, but how boring life gets. Oh, for the days of gardening and sewing, for my little children at my knees," cries Bessie. "I wish I could have a break from the monotony of my life."

"Larry, wake up. Will you turn me over onto my other side?" asks handicapped Becky once again.

Larry answers with a weary sigh, "In sickness and in health, through thick and thin, but really it seems like in sickness and in sickness, through thin and thin. But, yes, I'll help you again."

Morning arrived for Larry and Becky. Nights could seem hard, but the mornings seemed even harder. Gone were the days of getting up to a steaming, hot breakfast. Now it was hurry, scurry. Where are the clean jeans? Who would iron Kari's dress? How could they make it without Becky's care?

Linda wiped her eyes. "What could be harder than losing one's spouse at such a young age?" It seemed overwhelming to raise the children alone, to train them in the right way, to feed and clothe them. The task was more than she could bear. Could she go on?

Weary traveler, do not give up. Do not be a quitter, for Jesus says, "...he that endureth to the end shall be saved" (Matt. 10:22). Some other words to be comforted by are: "Consider it pure joy, my brothers, whenever you face trials of many kinds, because you know that the testing of your faith develops perseverance" (James 1:2,3, NIV).

No matter what our age or what we may be called to endure, we must remain strong to the end. The land of promise is for the warrior in Christ, for those who endure, those who never quit or never give up.

To Love a Child

The telephone rings, and Kim thinks, "Is it a friend, or is it the social worker calling to say we must come to the court hearing deciding our daughter's fate?"

She is not our blood daughter, but she is our daughter in our hearts. If one would have seen her the day we got her, then would look at her now, you could not help but say we loved her like our own. Does not that have something to say? "Please, Lord, let us keep her."

The dreaded day came when their fears became reality. "Oh, Lord, walk with us in the days to come when we are lonesome for those dear little arms to encircle our necks, to hear a sweet voice say, 'Mommy, Daddy, I love you!' " cried Martin and Kimberly. "Lord, we saw Kursten take her first steps. we heard her lisp her first prayer. We know she was comforted at night with her teddy bear and one more drink of water. Who will know that she loved to hear 'Jesus Loves Me' before going to sleep? Who will tell her now that Jesus loves her? Our questions may never be answered. Will the holes in our hearts ever be healed? Oh, Lord, You cannot understand the heartache."

"Son, daughter, I do understand. I gave My Son, My only Son, to a sin-cursed world. I know the hurt of giving up your loved one, to not be able to cradle that dear one in your arms when you know he or she is hurting or lonely. Remember that I want to enfold you in my arms when you have a lump in your throat and you are lonesome. Remember, too, that I love Kursten. My eyes see her. I want you to know that I am caring for her. I want her to be saved even more than you want it."

"Father, You do understand. You know our every heartache. We know we can fly to Your arms for comfort. We commit our darling baby to You, knowing that You love her even more than we do."

The Caregiver

Loren and Frances were happily married. Then tragedy struck, and Frances became a handicapped person. Frances was not the only one who suffered, for her family suffered, too. Loren and their daughter, Sophia, were the caregivers and shared most in the suffering. No, they were not in a wheelchair, nor did they suffer the any number of things handicapped people suffer, but yet sometimes the load was heavy. It was difficult to see their loved one lose her strength and the ability to do so many household jobs she had loved to do.

Frances knew her loved ones struggled with this burden. Often times her friends or church family would tell her, "I'm praying for you," and she was always grateful for their words of concern and encouragement.

One day Frances considered how her life had been when she was healthy. Had she helped to lift some other's load, whether they were handicapped or a caregiver? She realized it is easier to remember someone in prayer when you see the need everyday. But when it was not as obvious, had she prayed for others, imploring God to grant mercy and to extend grace for the needs? Had she thanked God for the goodness and courage He sent to the suffering one or to the caregiver? Now, more than before, she knew the need for prayer.

"...pray one for another, that ye may be healed. The effectual fervent prayer of a righteous man availeth much" (James 5:16).

Grief and Tears

The Bible says there is "A time to weep...a time to mourn" (Eccles. 3:4). God does not ask us to not cry. He knows our griefs are real. In fact, He tells us to "weep with them that weep" (Rom. 12:15). Furthermore, He showed us it is all right to cry when we suffer loss—He cried at the grave of his friend Lazarus.

Some verses on grief and tears are: "I am weary with my groaning; all the night make I my bed to swim; I water my couch with my tears. Mine eye is consumed because of grief..." (Ps. 6:6,7).

Thanks be to God for the next verses: "The righteous cry, and the Lord heareth and delivereth them out of all their trouble" (Ps. 34:17) "...weeping may endure for a night, but joy cometh in the morning" (Ps. 30:5). Praise God for the morning!

The most grand morning will be when we step ashore and find ourselves at home where God Himself will wipe the tears from our eyes. "And God shall wipe away all tears from their eyes; and there shall be no more death, neither sorrow, nor crying, neither shall there be any more pain: for the former things are passed away" (Rev. 21:4).

The Bond of Perfectness

"And above all these things put on charity, which is the bond of perfectness" (Col. 3:14).

"Jesus loves me, this I know," sang Bonita to comfort her nine-month-old daughter, Julie. "Sometimes when your baby is ill, time seems to crawl so slowly," Bonita mused to herself as she laid the sleeping Julie in her crib.

But time did not stand still. Before long Julie was eating by herself, and Bonita was sweeping the crumbs off the floor that Julie dropped. "Oh, Julie, need you spill your water every time you eat?" moaned Bonita. "Sometimes it seems I spend my time mopping up or sweeping the floor behind you." There were many happy times, though. Mother and daughter spent time reading, playing games, and singing together.

Soon, so soon, Bonita was admonishing Julie, "Stand still while I comb your hair for school." Before long, Julie was able to read to Mom. There were lots of ways Julie was growing up.

When Julie started the second grade, it became obvious that something was wrong with her mother. She started being protective of her mother, offering her help and encouragement in many ways. It was fun to learn to comb her own hair, to help with the cooking, to do more "grown up," tasks in the house. But, oh, this worrisome something that plagued them all.

They found out there was a name for the malady that bothered Mom. It was very real and would never go away. Julie vowed she would always be there for Mom. It was easy, even though she was now a big girl (all of ten years old!) to hold her mother's hand because "Mom stumbles a lot." Mother and daughter discovered a new way of doing something special together. It was fun to have a tea party once a week, a time to talk and share together. They decided this was one thing they would always do.

As time went on, Julie became more and more responsible for the housekeeping for the family of five. It was not always fun anymore. Then Julie met the Lord. What a great mystery to have Heaven's peace. Now she had Someone who could really understand her struggles. "Oh, bond of heaven's union!"

How hard it was to be the main housekeeper. She was sweeping crumbs from the floor that Mom dropped, she was wiping up water spills and combing Mom's hair. Such a short time ago, Mom had done these things for her. Praise the Lord for His love; their hearts were being knit together with cords of love.

Mom discovered there was something special she could do for Julie and that was to keep Julie company as she went from room to room working. What they had begun in their tea parties, talking and sharing, now became a part of their daily life. When one was down or discouraged, the other one would encourage and lift her spirits. Bonita and Julie learned to accept each other and Bonita's limitations, thereby living so as to please God.

Anxiety of Suffering

Karen sat in her wheelchair with a look of despair on her face. She had been bound to this disease for ten long years, and how many more would there be? A look of fear was in her eyes; would she be able to hold on? But she had no alternatives; she wanted a heavenly home. Life was discouraging, though. She bowed her head in prayer. "Lord, I am so weak and frail. I am tired of sitting in my wheelchair, tired of not being able to care for my family, but, most of all, I'm tired of not being able to care for myself. Too, I have fears of the time when I will lose more physical strength. I do not have the power to carry this burden. And then, Lord, what of my loved ones? I know they have an equally heavy load. They are human, too, and get weary. And, Father, how could I bear it if their love should fail? Oh, Lord, please help me cope; I am so weak. '...according to thy mercy remember thou me for thy goodness' sake' " (Ps. 25:7).

"My grace is sufficient for thee; for my strength is made perfect in weakness" (1 Cor. 12:9). "It is of the Lord's mercies that we are not consumed, because his compassions fail not. They are new every morning: great is thy faithfulness" (Lam. 3:22,23). "...and, lo, I am with you always, even unto the end of the world" (Matt. 28:20). "As the Father hath loved me, so have I loved you..." (John 15:9). "The eternal God is thy refuge, and underneath are the everlasting arms..." (Deut. 33:27). "And, behold, I am with thee, and will keep thee in all places whither thou goest..." (Gen. 28:15).

"Father, how good You are to me!" "Thou art worthy, O Lord, to receive glory and honour and power..." (Rev. 4:11). "Oh, that men would praise the Lord for his goodness, and for his wonderful works to the children of men!" (Ps. 107:8). "...he is altogether lovely. This is my beloved, and this is my friend..." (Song of Sol. 5:16).

"But I am poor and needy; yet the Lord thinketh upon me: thou art my help and my deliverer..." (Ps. 40:17). Praise the Lord!

"The Lord is my shepherd; I shall not want" (Ps. 23:1). "O my God, I trust in thee..." (Ps. 25:2).

Christian Qualities

"And have put on the new man, which is renewed in knowledge after the image of him that created him" (Col. 3:10).

My brother once told me, "The more we decrease physically, the more we must increase spiritually." To know that even though we may be physically incapacitated, we can grow spiritually should be an encouragement to us.

May we take courage from each other and continue to grow daily. A caregiver once said, "My patient is always so thankful for what I do for her. As I am in the process of helping her, she is already expressing her thanks."

A daughter said of her father, "In spite of the fact that he is weakening, he is always upbeat and cheerful."

In speaking of my uncle, who is now deceased, my cousin said, "Even though Dad could not see, he never complained. Once as I was describing the sunset to him, he didn't even remind me of how he used to enjoy them."

Another sadly disabled person, who has passed away, had this spoken of her, "She gave the Lord much honor in her great love for Him in spite of what she was called to bear."

When a missionary family came home, they said they had really enjoyed the letters from blind Hannah. She not only wrote news but would often include a quiz or riddle for the children.

A minister spoke this of one of his deceased parishioners, "She suffered much and was ready to go home to her Creator, but I will miss her, as I know she prayed often for me."

A mother says this of her disabled son, "Though he cannot run and play as other children, he is always happy. He sings like a bird, lifting our spirits often."

May we look at the qualities of those bearing the ministry of suffering and make them our own, becoming more and more like Jesus. "I press toward the mark for the prize of the high calling of God in Christ Jesus" (Phil. 3:14).

Disabled, Beauty, and Acceptance

Sixteen-year-old Sue glanced in the mirror. She was slender and flaxen haired, but she groaned. Why did she have to have skin problems? Her best friend had smooth, clear skin and was so well accepted by the rest of their peers. Beauty was definitely "in."

Jill groaned. She had such a weight problem. She felt like she just needed to smell food and she gained weight. Her friend, Tasha was slender and definitely "in."

Twenty-year-old Jason flexed his muscles. He struggled with the thought of how puny he always looked when he stood beside Thomas at youth activities. Strong was the "in" thing.

Tiny, petite Tara knew she was not good at volleyball. Why could not she be just a little bit taller so she could flick the ball over the net? Athletic was so "in."

Two little tow-haired boys ran up to Sue, a slender, young woman in a wheelchair, and, laughing, said, "You must be too fat to walk." Then they innocently tumbled on. Running by her again, they pointed their fingers at her and laughed. She kindly called them to come to her and, putting her arms about them, told them how at one time she was able to run and play like they were. But now God had a different plan for her. They asked questions about life as a handicapped person and were soon walking away, two sober little boys.

Sue was glad to be out in the glorious day while her husband, Ralph, pushed her wheelchair around the lake. They had taken a bag of bread crumbs along to feed the ducks. While they were feeding the ducks, a disfigured duck came to grab a few bites, too. Ralph said, "Someone needs to get rid of that ugly duckling."

"Why, Ralph, why do you say that?" questioned Sue.

"Because he is one ugly, sad-looking duck," replied her husband.

"Is that any reason for doing away with a creature, because they don't match up to our standard?" questioned Sue. "If one needs to be beautiful or perfect to be accepted, where would one who is handicapped come in?"

She continued to ponder the thought of acceptance in society. She well remembered how inferior she felt in her youth because she had a skin problem. Was tall, slender, young, strong, and healthy the way to be "in"? Could one not be wholly accepted or feel accepted unless they measured up?

As Sue took these questions to Jesus, she received this comforting thought, "When one belongs to the King and is His son or daughter, why should he or she feel inferior? Jesus loves us all the same."

"Behold, what manner of love the Father hath bestowed upon us, that we should be called the sons of God" (1 John 3:1). "God, who is rich in mercy, for his great love wherewith he loved us" (Eph. 2:4). "Unto me, who am less than the least of all saints, is this grace given...the unsearchable riches of Christ" (Eph. 3:8).

Calamity—Good or Bad?

Wesley was pleased with his wheat crop. Give it one more month and there should be a good harvest. With one more glance, he turned to go into the house for breakfast. He was anxious to share his pleasure in the crop with Carolyn. She understood him so well.

A week passed. Then one morning the sky was cloudy, and by noon a north wind had picked up. Wesley glanced at the sky anxiously. He hurried into the house for lunch and told his fears to Carolyn. When they bowed their heads to thank God for the noon meal, Wesley also asked God to protect their farm from calamity.

When he stepped out of the house after lunch, he gave the sky a quick appraisal. Things did not look good. It really was no surprise when it started to hail later in the afternoon. In fifteen minutes, it was all over, and Wesley got into his pickup to assess the damage.

When he came into the house, Wesley looked grief stricken. He told Carolyn they had lost at least half of the crop. Wesley said he felt like he must be a sinful man and surely God had allowed this to punish him.

Carolyn was quiet for awhile, wondering what to say to help Wesley. Then she said, "Wes, we live in this world where these things happen. It rains on the just and unjust. What matters is how we react to it. The devil wants these calamities to happen so we will become discouraged, but God knows these disappointments can work a peaceable fruit of righteousness in us. The devil always has evil in mind, but God takes these things and turns them into good.

"When Jesus was crucified, the devil was delighted to see the suffering of Jesus, and he was more pleased yet when he saw the terrible deed completed. He felt like he had won the victory. God took this terrible deed, though, and turned it into salvation's plan for all mankind! If we will only let our heartaches and disappointments work in our favor, then we will come out the winner."

"Though he slay me, yet will I trust in him..." (Job 13:15).

Allowing Faith to Grow

Layne was fearful. What did his life hold for him? He had broken his back in an automobile accident and was paralyzed from his waist down. How would he be able to cope? But what if he died? Where would he be? He had so many tiring questions and no place to go for answers.

While lying in the rehabilitation hospital, he heard a commotion in the hallway one night. Soon he was hearing the most beautiful singing. He listened very carefully to the words; they were beautiful words, but new to him. He heard songs of God's love, songs of Heaven and peace. How he longed for peace. Soon a gentleman stepped into his room. He had a look of peace, and what was it? Joy on his face? After a short friendly visit, his visitor was gone.

Two weeks later, on Sunday afternoon, Layne awakened to hear the singing he had heard before. Would Mr. Troyer step in to see him again? He hoped so. He wanted to ask him what his secret was, why he looked so happy and peaceful. Mr. Troyer did remember him, and when he left, Layne had some new and interesting thoughts to think on.

The next visit Mr. Troyer paid Layne, he gave him a Bible. When he left, Layne had many sober and serious thoughts. He remembered the accident and was very thankful he was still living. He realized God had been merciful to him in sparing his life. He was thankful that Edwin had brought him a Bible. He longed to have peace and joy in his heart.

Two weeks later Edwin stepped into Room 505 and started to back out right away. The man in bed opened his eyes and immediately called a cheery hello to Edwin. With a look of surprise on his face, Edwin went to the bed.

"Layne, you look so different I did not recognize you. Will you tell me what has happened?" asked Edwin. Then followed two hours of joyful sharing. When Edwin left, he marveled at Layne's joy in the Lord.

Several months later Edwin noticed a subtle change in Layne. He was not as happy as before. Upon questioning Layne, Edwin discovered that he had a fear of the future. Edwin realized some of this was normal for one whose physical life had gone through such a change. But when, on subsequent visits, Layne was still down, Edwin felt he should address the problem.

He told Layne he enjoyed birds. He then asked him if had ever seen a cowbird. When Layne answered that he had not, Edwin described them. He told him that a cowbird does not build her own nest. She picks a nest of a smaller bird; then she will lay her egg in that nest with another's eggs in it. When the other bird comes back, she will set on her nest to hatch her eggs. When the eggs have hatched, there is one nestling that is larger and more aggressive than the others. Because of this, he gets most of the food, and the other nestlings starve to death.

"How dreadful!" exclaimed Layne.

"That is what is happening in your own life," Edwin said. "The enemy has planted the spirit of fear and worry in your heart. This spirit is very aggressive and demands your attention. Therefore you are not allowing the fruit of trust, praise, and faith to grow."

Layne bowed his head, sighing a prayer of repentance to his Savior and promising to give Him his worries and fears.

How is it in your life? Which spirit are you feeding most often? Whatsoever things are true, honest, just, pure, lovely, think on these things (Phil. 4:8).

Longing for Home, and Learning

"I wish I could go home to Heaven," I sighed wearily to our daughter.

"Mom, you should not say that, " she admonished. "Your work is not finished here. If it were, the Lord would take you home. Remember our friend who was here last week? I know you really love him and pray often for him."

"I do," I acknowledged.

"Well, maybe there are not many others praying for him, and he needs you here," she said.

We long to go home because of our suffering, but would we long for Heaven if it were not for suffering? Our suffering is a means to draw us closer to God. "Come unto me, all ye that labour and are heavy laden, and I will give you rest" (Matt. 11:28).

Suffering teaches us to have complete dependence on God. "Casting all your care upon him; for he careth for you" (1 Pet. 5:7).

Suffering teaches obedience. "...yet learned he obedience by the things which he suffered"(Heb. 5:8).

Suffering teaches trust and assurance. "He giveth power to the faint; and to them that have no might he increaseth strength" (Isa. 40:29). "I the Lord have called thee...and will hold thine hand, and will keep thee..." (Isa.42:6).

"The eternal God is thy refuge, and underneath are the everlasting arms: and he shall thrust out the enemy from before thee..." (Deut. 33:27).

Now we can say, "Though he slay me, yet will I trust in him..." (Job 13:15).

We also learn patience. "...knowing that tribulation worketh patience" (Rom. 5:3).

Because suffering has taught us patience, obedience, trust, and faith, we now long for Heaven, because we love God and want to be eternally with Him. We can now say, "For me to live is Christ, and to die is gain" (Phil. 1:21).

Time Spent, but How?

"What a hectic day I've had," said Wanda. She enumerated the many activities she had been busy with. "In between loads of laundry, I canned two bushels of peaches and went for some parts for Roland. How have you spent your day, Rita?"

Mentally I ticked off my day's activities. There was no way it could possibly compare to Wanda's busy schedule. Briefly I told of my day. "I went from room to room in my wheelchair while our daughter cleaned the house; I was keeping her company. Then when she went grocery shopping, I had a nap. Later I wrote a letter to friends who are missionaries in the Philippines."

A few days later a friend called, saying, "I need a break from sewing Shayla's school dresses, so I thought I would give you a call. What have you been doing today?"

Again I wondered what I could say. How would it sound to say I had spent extra time reading God's Word and other good literature, but what else could I say? So I spoke of just that.

One day my aunt from a distant state called. Kindly she asked, "Rita, does your time get long and wearisome?"

I could honestly answer, "Not usually. I have letters to write, good literature to read, and there are so many to pray for, friends and family, the leaders of our church and country and whoever the Holy Spirit asks me to remember."

Then one day while reading from the Bible, I read, "Son [Daughter], go work to day in my vineyard" (Matt. 21:28). God had called me to a different work than some.

Later I read, "Whereas ye know not what shall be on the morrow. For what is your life? It is even a vapour, that appeareth for a little time, and then vanisheth away" (James 4:14).

Reading this scripture brought another one to my mind, 1 Corinthians 9:24-27: "Know ye not that they which run in a race run all, but one receiveth the prize? So run, that ye may obtain...Now they do it to obtain a corruptible crown; but we an incorruptible. I therefore so run, not as uncertainly; so fight I, not as one that beateth the air: But I keep under my body, and bring it into subjection..."

I am called to a ministry of suffering (an agent of distress), but life is only a vapor and will soon vanish away. I need to run with patience the race that is set before me so I can receive the prize, the incorruptible crown.

Shattered Lives and Dreams, and God's Love

"The Lord is good, a strong hold in the day of trouble; and he knoweth them that trust in him"(Nah. 1:7).

There is a breed of cat called a Tuxedo cat. They are beautiful black cats with white aprons under their chins, white mittens or socks on their fore-paws and white knee-length socks on their back legs. They make a good pet, as generally they are well behaved, not demanding, very clean and particular.

Our daughter and son have a Tuxedo cat. But he had a traumatic experience in his life, and his personality has changed. He is still beautiful, but he is more demanding and not as careful with his cleanliness. This makes no difference to his masters. He is still loved and very much wanted.

Sometimes our emotions, spirits, or feelings can be like this, mostly dark but with enough white so that no one suspects much is wrong. Then one day something goes wrong; a traumatic experience happens. Our personality changes. Our emotions and feelings have changed. Our loved ones no longer understand us, and, worse yet, we no longer understand ourselves.

Should this be happening in your life, you can be assured that your loved ones still love you. God loves you. He always has and always will. "Behold, what manner of love the Father hath bestowed upon us..." (1 John 3:1).

In a large retirement center in the southwest, most of the lawns are rock, not grass. However, there is one yard that is neither rock or grass. It is covered with broken glass. Upon hearing this, one wonders at such a yard. Surprisingly, it looks rather pretty. When the sun shines on the broken glass, it sparkles and shines.

So when our lives and dreams have been broken, God, with His loving touch, can cause them to shine again. With His love, He is able to produce a thing of beauty out of our shattered lives. We may feel we have a right to question why. But God does not owe any of us an answer. He is supreme, and we have His Word with its many promises. "The Lord will give you, according as he hath promised..." (Exod. 12:25).

A dear friend who has gone through dark and troublesome times told me recently he worries about falling away from the grace of God at the end of his life. A verse to remember when the devil torments one with these thoughts is, "Wherefore he is able also to save them to the uttermost that come unto God by him, seeing he ever liveth to make intercession for them" (Heb. 7:25).

To Win a Crown

Gloria, who had multiple sclerosis, was attempting to get from her bed to her wheelchair. She fell and landed between the footrests, causing the wheelchair to collapse on top of her. It was not only uncomfortable but it was painful. She wore a call button to get help, and she managed to press it on her way down.

While Gloria was waiting for someone to come to her aid, she started talking to Jesus, saying, "Lord, I know You are wanting my attention. I want to be open to You. Do You have someone for me to pray for? Do you want me to praise You in spite of calamity, or do You have a lesson, a special message for me?"

After a moment of stillness and peacefulness, this was the impression she received: "Am I a soldier of the cross, A foll'wer of the Lamb?...Must I be carried to the skies On flow'ry beds of ease, While others fought to win the prize, And sailed thro' bloody seas?...Sure I must fight, if I would reign; Increase my courage, Lord; I'll bear the toil, endure the pain, Supported by Thy Word...Wear a crown, wear a crown, Wear a bright and shining crown...And when the battle's over we shall wear a crown in the New Jerusalem." *

This was an awesome lesson, An overwhelming thankfulness that God so graciously heard and answered her prayer with this song gave Gloria much joy. It was easy to sing this song and praise God while waiting for a neighbor to come help her.

Are we willing to suffer, to bear our cross? Or do we think, I do not deserve this burden the Lord has given me?

We shall wear a crown if we endure to the end. Praise the Lord!

Encouragement

Encouragement

I wish you to be successful in your Christian life. I want you to have a home in Heaven.

In Isaiah 30:15, we read, "...in quietness and in confidence shall be your strength." As we take advantage of the grace God gives us, He accepts us. When we obey as the Holy Spirit brings convictions to us, we grow. Disobedience causes us to become weaker and weaker. When you have choices to make, always stand up for the right.

"Every morning mercies new..." Each day the slate is clean, so thank Him for the times He has blessed you, and He will bless you again. An attitude of gratitude is a must and helps us through the rough times. When you have done your best, God will do the rest. He loves us so much and wants us saved even more than we want salvation.

When we are tempted with bad thoughts, it helps to bury ourselves in good reading material, which is a steppingstone to successful Christian living. Poor reading material is a drain and not conducive to spiritual health. We need to be acquainted with our Father, as we are going to see Him and want to spend eternity with Him.

Ask the Lord if He has anything for you to do. Then, though I might sound like a broken record, follow in obedience.

The devil leaves no one out when it comes to temptations! He is cruel and is the father of lies. So when we have things we have repented of but yet the scars and memories remain, we need to remember, "...whatsoever things are of good report; if there be any virtue, and if there be any praise, think on these things" (Phil. 4:8).

Do not be ashamed to share your struggles with a trusted friend. When you see a friend in need, do not hesitate to give encouragement, for in so doing, we grow also.

A Bible verse to have in our memory is, "Fear thou not: for I am with thee; be not dismayed; for I am thy God: I will strengthen thee; yea, I will uphold thee with the right hand of my righteousness" (Isa. 41:10).

New Year

Once a young lady worked in the kitchen at a retirement home. Just before the New Year, she was given a clipboard and pencil and asked to go into the storage room and make inventory. She needed to write down all the supplies and how much there was of each item. This way it was known what to order and how much or what was more than needed. It was also recorded what was not used or what needed to be discarded.

Now is a good time to stop and ponder our lives, to take inventory of our lives. Do we have a good supply of praise and adoration, gentleness, love, thankfulness, all the fruit of the Spirit?

Maybe we will find arrogance, self-honor, unthankfulness, or other items that need to be discarded. Possibly in a dark corner, we will need to take a flashlight (God's Word) and do a soul search, thus revealing a need for cleansing.

Then when we are emptied and clean, we need to take care that we fill the "storage area," our hearts and minds, with "whatsoever things are lovely."

Joy versus Trials

Let us consider this verse, "My brethren, count it all joy when ye fall into divers temptations; knowing this, that the trying of your faith worketh patience. But let patience have her perfect work, that ye may be perfect and entire, wanting nothing" (James 1:2,3). In other words, consider it pure joy whenever you face trials, because you know that the testing of your faith develops strength. A trial is not just a struggle to be borne, but it is a chance to prove your love to God and make your faith stronger.

God may test you, and the devil may tempt you, but you will decide the outcome. You can choose to go either forward or backward.

We will be less likely to sin if we realize that sin breaks God's heart. The sin of one of His children hurts God more than the sin of a sinner.

Every day we must be in the fight for our salvation. We need to arm ourselves with the armor of God: a bulletproof vest of prayer, the shield of faith, our trust in God, the shining sword, which is the sword of the Spirit and the Word of God. Let us not forget to sing a song of praise, and when we have been victorious, let us sing the song of victory.

Someday we will be able to say, "I've fought a good fight, I've kept the faith..."

We cannot expect Christian life to "just happen." We need to make total commitments and exercise obedience. Then and then only can we expect power and strength in our lives for when the hard times come. God's power, His energy, flows through us the moment we exercise faith for a given task. "I can do all things through Christ which strengtheneth me" (Phil. 4:13).

"Only fear the Lord, and serve him in truth with all your heart: for consider how great things he hath done for you" (1 Sam. 12:24).

Prodigal Son

I have thought of the prodigal son. He was dearly loved, and yet he wanted "out." He wanted to try his own wings.

Too many times, this is also how it is with us. We are sons and daughters, dearly loved, but we turn our backs on God, wasting our lives. We "do our own thing," going our own selfish way. We ignore God and waste the wonderful resources He has provided for us.

The devil wraps his web tighter and tighter around us. Without realizing it, we are in slavery to him. We are on a downward path which leads to destruction and death, eternal death.

After the prodigal son had wasted his life, when he looked up and came to his senses, he said, "I will arise and return to my father."

The father was watching the road for his son's return.

Our Father is watching and longing for us to return to Him when we have been wayward. His compassion and love are sure. He has not turned His back on us, nor has He forgotten us. We are still His children, howbeit wayward.

Though we turn our backs on God, His intentions are always good toward us. He wants us saved more than we want to be saved. The minute we turn towards Him, He is there waiting for us with open arms. He is waiting to forgive and accept us. He longs to reclaim and restore us to our rightful position as His son or daughter.

Each time a soul is saved, the angels ring their bells. Have they rung for you?

A Stretcher Bearer

We feel concerned and sometimes are frustrated when we have a loved one going astray. There are many tears shed, which God understands. He hears them when they fall; so take courage.

In Luke 5, we read of the friends removing tiles from the roof and letting their friend down to Jesus for healing. Their faith and commitment to an Almighty God caused them to do this. We should have this same faith and commitment when we become a "stretcher bearer" for our loved one.

Removing the tiles would be confessing my faults or removing any barrier that would stand between Jesus and me. Then I can present my loved one to Him on a stretcher, prayer. This will be a great source of comfort to us if we bring our loved one to the Father each morning. It releases us of the burden that "he must change." Only the power of God can bring our loved ones to salvation. Sometimes we would like to be the one to bring conviction to our dear one, but that is the work of the Holy Spirit.

Some Bible verses that are precious at this time are: 2 Chronicles 20:15, 17: "Be not afraid nor dismayed by reason of this great multitude [problem]; for the battle is not yours but God's. Ye shall not need to fight in this battle: set yourselves, stand ye still, and see the salvation of the Lord..." 2 Corinthians 10:4: "For the weapons of our warfare are not carnal, but mighty through God to the pulling down of strong holds."

Our work at this time is to show love to the erring one. We serve such a mighty God, and we should not doubt Him. We are so frail and human; it is easy for us to pick up the burden of an unsaved one going lost.

A couple of verses to read and practice are Psalm 149:5 and 6: "Let the saints be joyful in glory; let them sing aloud upon their beds [troubles] Let the high praises of God be in their mouth, and a two-edged sword [promises of God] in their hand."

I will put my trust in God and will not carry a burden; rather I will be full of praises. Then I will truly be able to take a hold of the pallet of my dear one and put it down where peace and safety abide.

Forgiveness

Do you wish to be free from the poison of sin in your life? To be able to start a new life? To be free of sin's poison, you must take an honest look at yourself, repent and confess your sin, turning your back on it. This is a lifeline for you.

I read, "Neither do I condemn thee: go, and sin no more" (John 8:11). Jesus is offering you the golden scepter, the scepter of forgiveness and love.

The Pharisees came haughtily and boldly, pulling and shoving the woman. They had caught her in "the very act." This is like the evil one is to us, saying, "You're had now. There is no hope for you."

What would Jesus have to say now? The Law said she should be stoned. And so does the Law condemn each one of us. Rubbing their hands gleefully, the Pharisees waited for Jesus to uphold the Law. He said nothing.

Instead He stooped down and started writing in the sand. The Pharisees waited, perhaps not very patiently. Their curiosity was piqued, "What is this Man writing?" And they strained to see. Do you think He could have been writing a list of their sins?

He continued writing, but breaking the silence, He said, "Let him that hath no sin cast the first stone."

Raising Himself, He found her alone. He looked at her tenderly and with compassion. (He has this compassion for us, too.) He asked, "Where are thy accusers? Hath none condemned thee?"

She wept as she answered, "None, Lord."

He said softly, "Neither do I condemn thee. Go, and sin no more." She felt clean and free. Her desire for wanton living was gone. In its place, she now felt self-respect and a desire to serve this new Master.

So He is saying to you and me, "Neither do I condemn thee. Go, and sin no more." No matter what our condemnation, the Lord grants forgiveness— not a stoning.

Nuggets of Gold

As I was walking (figuratively speaking) along the sandy shores of life today, I occasionally would see a glimmer, something shiny in the sand. I stooped to pick up these glimmering objects and, upon examining them, found them to be nuggets of gold which I want to share with you.

David writes in Psalm 34:5, "Those who look to him are radiant; their faces are never covered with shame" (NIV). When God forgives, we need never feel embarrassed or ashamed of anything that has happened, because we have become a child of the King. Forgive yourself, and go on with living.

"The righteous cry, and the Lord heareth, and delivereth them out of all their troubles" (Ps. 34:17). That is a wonderful promise. The Lord has a way for us in all our questions; He promises that He will be with us.

Some more nuggets of gold: Isaiah 43:1-3, "But now thus saith the Lord that created thee, O Jacob, and he that formed thee, O Israel, Fear not: for I have redeemed thee, I have called thee by thy name; thou art mine. When thou passeth through the waters, I will be with thee; and through the rivers, they shall not overflow thee: when thou walkest through the fire, thou shalt not be burned; neither shall the flame kindle upon thee. For I am the Lord thy God, the holy one of Israel, thy Saviour..." Is it any wonder that I call these "nuggets of gold"? Now go on to verse 4 of the same chapter, "Since thou wast precious in my sight, thou hast been honourable, and I have loved thee..."

The Bible is full of these nuggets of gold. Here are some more: Isaiah 40:29, 30, "He giveth power to the faint; and to them that have no might he increaseth strength. Even the youths shall faint and be weary, and the young men shall utterly fall." He knows we are weak and will fall, but verse 31 says, "But they that wait upon the Lord shall renew their strength; they shall mount up with wings as eagles; they shall run, and not be weary; and they shall walk, and not faint."

These are promises of pure gold.

Storm and Safety

One day in Jesus' ministry, He and His disciples needed to go to the other side of the lake. Upon entering the ship, He said, "Let us go over unto the other side of the lake" (Luke 8:22). So, in obedience, they launched forth. "But as they sailed he fell asleep: and there came down a storm of wind on the lake; and they were filled with water, and were in jeopardy" (verse 23). Being fearful, they awakened Jesus and said, "Master, master, we perish" (verse 24).

How like our Christian lives this scenario is. Jesus asks us to do a job for Him or to be a witness for Him. Maybe He asks us to bear the ministry of suffering. We enter the ship, take up the task in obedience, and endeavor to follow His will. Then one day we do not feel so fine. Before long, we are in a storm. We wonder where our Savior is. After all, we thought we were in the center of His will, trying to do His will. We struggle valiantly and try to stay in the battle. After a time, we become fearful and call mightily upon God and cry, "Jesus, I need Thee 'ere I perish."

"Then he arose, and rebuked the wind and the raging of the water: and they ceased and there was a calm. And he said unto them, Where is your faith?...for he commandeth even the winds and water, and they obey him" (verses 24 and 25).

When Jesus was in the boat with the disciples, would it have sunk? We answer, "No, it was impossible for the boat to sink, because Jesus was in it."

We struggle and are fearful, afraid we may sink, and we hardly have the strength to whisper, "Jesus, save me." Instantly He is by our side, saying, "Peace, be still." In faith, we look to Him, and the tempest, the raging, the storm ceases. There is calmness and peace.

With Him in your (or my) boat, can it sink? No, it cannot, because He is there! "Where is your [my] faith?" (verse 25).

Occasionally in a fierce battle, someone may say, "I cannot fight anymore. I cannot handle the struggle of Christian living. I will bail out of my boat; I give up." So over the side of the boat they jump, jumping to sure destruction, to death.

Friend, if this is you, do not jump. Jesus is nearby, waiting for you to ask Him to calm the storm. "...for he commandeth even the winds and water, and they obey him" (verse 25).

Submission to Our Husbands

Kari was thrilled. She was engaged to Wade and had six weeks to prepare for her wedding. And then she thought, I have more to prepare for than a wedding day. She had a marriage to prepare for, a lifelong commitment. She puzzled about how to prepare, then she thought to herself, I know. I will ask each of my aunts for some advice. I will get a notebook and write the answers in it, so I won't forget.

She wrote across the top page, "Advice for a Bride."

Aunt Lillian said, "After you and Wade have had your first tiff," then seeing the look on Kari's face, she had to laugh. She said, "Kari, at this point, I know it seems like that will never happen, but it does. When it does, make a sign that says, 'If you want your marriage to succeed, you must forgive.' Then tack it to the inside of a cupboard door. Next go the second mile, complimenting him for his good qualities."

The next time Kari saw Aunt Susieanne, she asked her for advice, and this was Aunt Susie's answer, "Help Wade to feel more than just accepted. He needs to feel loved. Never compare Wade to another. Do not be critical, and never dwell on Wade's weaknesses." Kari was taken aback. Wade have weaknesses? She did not know of any.

Aunt Mildred said, "We need to respect and honor our husbands. A Bible verse to remember is, '...and the wife see that she reverence her husband' (Eph. 5:33). The Bible says 'to reverence' and that means even if we don't think they are what we think they should be. When you respect Wade, he will know he is special to you."

Then Kari wrote to her Aunt Julia, asking her what she had to say to a newly-married wife. The answer was, "When there is a conflict between your wishes and Wade's wishes, you must submit, as the Bible says, 'Wives, submit yourselves unto your own husbands, as unto the Lord. For the husband is the head of the wife, even as Christ is the head of the church: and is the saviour of the body' (Eph. 5:22,23). Submission is obeying Wade even if you don't feel like he deserves it."

Aunt Pauline felt that if one cultivated the fruit of the Spirit in marriage, it would be a sure plus to a home. She quoted Galatians 5:22, "But the fruit of the Spirit is love, joy, peace, longsuffering, gentleness, goodness, faith, Meekness, temperance."

Kari wanted Aunt Hazel's advice, too, so she called her one day. Her thought was to show enthusiasm for Wade's suggestions and desires. Aunt Hazel said this was giving support to him.

By now Kari's mind was very busy with all she had heard, but she had several more aunts to talk to. Were there more things to learn?

Aunt Eunice answered the question with this thought, "Show appreciation to Wade by being thankful for the many things he does for you. We all need to know we are appreciated."

Aunt Ina and Aunt Grace suggested cultivating homemaking skills, saying an orderly house and beds made would help Wade keep his spirits up.

Aunt Verda and Aunt Della encouraged Kari to improve her cooking skills; a well-cooked meal and attractive table would soothe and comfort Wade when the times were rough.

Aunt Maryann said to be cheerful even when Kari did not feel like it.

Kari wondered what Aunt Neoma could add that would be new. Aunt Neoma said to do things together, like taking a walk or washing the car or baking cookies. She added that a good family practice was singing together.

Kari felt overwhelmed with all there was to learn and be. But Aunt Goldie reminded her to begin the day with God, asking Him to be her Guide.

God's Love

God had a beautiful home, and He and His only Son enjoyed it together. However, God was a God of love and wanted to share His love. Also, He wanted to share His beautiful home. So He said to His Son, "Let us make man so he can share in our splendor."

Jesus saw this as a great plan. He was an "only Son" and wanted brothers and sisters.

God could see, though, that as man would be a free moral agent, he would make wrong choices sometimes. God was so pure and holy, He would not be able to tolerate sin. Jesus became willing to die for His brothers and sisters. His blood would wash their sins away.

God made man, and so soon he fell. Oh, the pain this caused in Heaven. It was time to put the rescue plan into operation.

Can we imagine the joy of the angels as they were preparing for Jesus to come to earth? Now those wayward children would have a chance to enjoy Heaven after all.

It was with pleasure and great joy that the angel could announce His birth. In fact, the joy was so great that more angels came to share in this awesome news, saying, "Glory to God in the highest and on earth, peace, good will toward men." Surely man would enjoy this most precious Son of God.

The sorrow was overwhelming when the angels saw the disrespect Jesus received. He was so brutally and shamefully treated and killed that they hid their faces—even hanging a black cloud over the earth to blot it all out. He died so we can be born to live.

Oh, the somber faces of the watching angels, but then the hallelujahs as He arose with triumph over His foes. He arose so we can rise with Him to newness of life.

Jesus knew if He were to stay on this earth, He could not be with all men at all times, so His love constrained Him to go to His heavenly Father so the Holy Spirit could be poured out on all mankind. Now He whispers softly, "Follow Me; I'll guide thee home."

It is God's love and His pleasure that He calls us home. It is with sublime joy that Jesus, our Brother, welcomes us to His abode when we arrive there. Oh, the wonder of it all!

Resist and Flee

A young man went into a bookstore looking for a book to buy. While looking around, he came upon some magazines that looked enticing. He picked one up, and glancing through it, he was reminded of a conversation he had had with a friend. The friend told him that he had heard a sermon on the subject of resisting the devil. Not only should a person resist, but he should flee from the devil.

So he put the magazine down, turned around, and fled.

When the devil accosted Eve in the garden of Eden, how differently it would have turned out had she run when she heard a "strange voice." Instead she listened, looked, handled, and then sinned.

When the devil says, "Psst. Look this way," we need to turn and flee.

Brokenness

Our wills need to be broken so God can use us. He never will use us unless we become broken. This is why God allows suffering, to break our wills. Even Jesus became willing and obedient to the Father, being broken for the sins of the world.

There are several stories in the Bible where it took brokenness to accomplish a purpose. When Jesus was feeding the five thousand, He broke the loaves and gave to the disciples, and they gave to the crowds. There was the young woman who broke the alabaster box so she could anoint the feet of Jesus.

The broken one is the one who can give in, the one who loses his self-right identity, the one who loses his pride. When we are broken, we can truly repent and walk in the light.

A saint in Heaven is a sinner who has been broken and has truly repented, thereby becoming a saint on earth. Hallelujah, that can be you and me.

Prayer

Linda gave her friend, June, a call on the telephone. She proceeded to give June a full report of the evening before when they had been invited to a picnic at the park for some out-of-state friends. About fifteen minutes later, Linda was still talking when June's baby awoke from her nap. The baby was contented in her crib for awhile, but after another fifteen minutes, she started getting fussy. June mentioned the baby waking up when there was a lull in the conversation, but the subject changed, and the talk continued.

June knew the baby was getting hungry and needed attention, but she could not get a word in. Finally she put the phone down, walked over, picked up the baby, changed her diaper, and went back to the phone. Linda was still talking.

That evening for devotions, Steve, June's husband, read 1 Samuel 3. As he read verse 9, where Eli instructed Samuel to tell the Lord, "Speak, Lord; for thy servant heareth," June thought of Linda and her conversation. She wondered if Linda prayed to the Lord the way she visited with her friends. Did Linda talk nonstop to God, make requests of Him, using Him as a listening post and an errand boy. Did Linda give the Lord a chance to talk to her? June wanted to be able to say to the Lord, "Speak, Lord; for thy servant heareth."

Unfinished Business

Abe had given his heart to God when he was but a lad. He was so thankful for the companionship he shared with his Maker. And now Abe was living in the Four Seasons Nursing Home, and there were days when he felt lonesome for Chester, his son. He was thankful when Chester called. Occasionally Chester would breeze in and ask, "How are you, Dad? Do you need anything?"

How could Abe explain that sometimes he would like a heart-to-heart visit? He would like to share with Chester what God had done and was doing for him.

Then one morning Chester received a phone call, "Come as soon as you are able. Your father has had a heart attack."

Immediately Chester dressed, and he drove quickly to the hospital. It was important he get to the hospital. When had he last told Dad that he loved him? When was the last heart-to-heart visit they shared? Oh, if only he had been more patient, more understanding. If only...

At last Chester arrived at the hospital. He was brusque with the nurses and doctors—after all, his father had to live. Chester had unfinished business. With this, Chester's life turned completely around. No longer was his business the number one concern, nor was his social life of such great importance that he could not be there for Dad.

Little by little Abe improved. It was a grand day when Chester was able to stay in Dad's room a few extra minutes and say, "Dad, I love you, and I'm sorry I've been so wrapped up in my life, not being here for you. Will you forgive me?"

Then there was the day Dad was stronger, he explained to Chester how God has a way of forgiving our failures, how God is patient with the weakest, most miserable sinners. He also explained that God wants our best and will not tolerate sin.

It was with a penitent heart that Chester could come to God and receive forgiveness for his sins. Now he had a joy and peace that passed all understanding.

How is it in your heart? Do you have any unfinished business?

Treasures in Earthen Vessels

"But we have this treasure in earthen vessels, that the excellency of the power may be of God, and not of us"(2 Cor. 4:7).

We have a plain jar on top of our dryer, and our daughter drops in it the quarters, nickels, and dimes she finds when she is doing the laundry. Sometimes when I pass by the dryer, I wonder why we do not get a prettier container for this change.

We have a special pitcher we use for our savings—the money from the jar goes into the pitcher. Possibly we are saving for a long-awaited trip to see our parents. How about the box in which we save the treasures our little ones bring us?

God also places treasures in unlikely containers. He puts His treasures in the poor, handicapped, simple, or ordinary. When we let Him pour His treasures into our hearts, we become a special vessel to Him that will bring Him honor and glory.

His splendor and beauty are best seen in the humble.

"Forgive as I Forgive You"

We read, "Verily I say unto you, All sins shall be forgiven unto the sons of men, and blasphemies wherewith soever they shall blaspheme: But he that shall blaspheme against the Holy Ghost hath never forgiveness, but is in danger of eternal damnation" (Mark 3:28,29).

Whatever has transpired, God has said that He will forgive anything except blasphemy against the Holy Ghost. Do you believe that?

Of course, there is a condition that needs to be met, and that is, "For if ye forgive men their trespasses, your heavenly Father will also forgive you: But if ye forgive not men their trespasses, neither will your Father forgive your trespasses" (Matt. 6:14,15).

Are you able to forgive? You say, "But there is never a change." Jesus said to forgive 490 times, and that was in one day. God is patient with us all. He never rushes through anything. If He were not patient, where would we be? God has a way of forgiving our failures. He is patient with the weakest, most miserable sinner.

If all conditions were met and we would become that "perfect one," God would take us home to Heaven because we are here to prepare to go there. Why be here any longer if we are ready for Heaven?

Wonder of all wonders, God loves us. He is generous, forgiving, and understanding. We need, in fact, we are commanded, to imitate Him and follow His example. Let us be as forgiving and loving to others as our Father is to us.

I Am a Housewife

I belong to a special sorority of sisters. I am a housewife.

Although my job pays well, often my billfold has only my driver's license in it. I am a housewife.

I love my boss, and he loves me. He shows his love by providing the same living for me as for himself. I am a housewife.

Some more ways I receive my pay is with love, contentment, joy, smiles, fun, and loyalty from my family. I am a housewife.

Together my boss and I have a Superior Being we answer to. He ordained our jobs, therefore they are not drudgery but of supreme importance. I am a housewife.

Like all other jobs, I owe my boss loyalty, but in this job I owe my boss more, I owe him submission. I am a housewife.

I love my job! Some call it common, but I know it is a noble one and has a high calling. I am a housewife.

As long as life permits, I will have only this one boss, for I will never change jobs for another. I am a housewife.

Therefore I need never be critical of my boss or dwell on his weaknesses. I am a housewife.

"Nevertheless let every one of you in particular so love his wife even as himself; and the wife see that she reverence her husband" (Eph. 5:33).

> Love is two hearts joined together by God
> Who care, share, and forgive one another.
> Thank You, O Father, for binding our hearts together.
>
> *Author of poem unknown*

Sounds of Home

Recently because of an illness, I spent hours at home in my recliner. One evening when the family was in church and I was home alone, I realized that there were certain comforting sounds, sounds that I was familiar with, that were giving me comfort and cheer. Some of these sounds were the cuckoo clock, refrigerator, wind chimes, a wall clock with a special tick, and others.

Then I thought of my eternal home. Could I hear sounds from "home" that were drawing me and warming my heart? Could I hear echoes of the angels singing? Can we hear family and friends "calling back" to us, urging us to be faithful? More important, can we hear our Father and Elder Brother urging us to be faithful a little longer?

May we always hear the comforting sounds of home.

Answered Prayers

Shawn was a cherished newborn. He had been a long awaited child. His parents took great delight in him, but his feet did not look normal. They were crooked; could something be wrong?

At Shawn's six-week checkup, the doctor said he would keep a close watch on the baby's feet to see how they grew. By the time he was three months old, the doctor said, "We need to make an appointment with a specialist about Shawn's feet."

So the specialist was visited, and when he pronounced Shawn's feet as being club feet, it brought much sorrow to the young parents' hearts. The first course of action was to have casts put on Shawn's feet to straighten them out. After three months of wearing casts, it was decided the baby could now wear shoes, but the left shoe would need to be on the right foot and the right shoe on the left foot.

What chagrin Shawn's mother felt when she was told time and again, "I don't mean to embarrass you, but you have your baby's shoes on the wrong feet."

After several months, another method was taken. This time Shawn's parents were told he would need to wear "straight last" shoes. Now what was that? They had never heard of those before. So after a trip to a special shoe store, straight last shoes were discovered to be shoes with no left or right.

Again it took patience and hope to see if these would take care of the problem, but after several months of wearing these special shoes, the doctor said, "Everything we have done has not worked. We will try braces, and if that does not work, the only alternative is surgery. Remember, Shawn must wear these braces for each nap and at night."

With heavy hearts, the parents took the braces home. Within a few hours, it was time for Shawn's first nap with the braces. But, alas, no matter how hard his mother tried, she could not get the braces on. She called Shawn's daddy, and he tried to get the braces on Shawn's feet. Soon they were all in tears. Then the father said, "I don't think we need these braces. Let us kneel down and ask God to heal."

In humility and simplicity, in faith in an almighty God, they did just that.

A few days shy of the next doctor's appointment, Shawn's mother took the braces back to the doctor and told him. "Our son has been healed. We do not need these anymore." Within several months, Shawn was walking. Now twenty-one years later, a person would never guess Shawn was born with club feet. Many times Shawn's parents have thanked the Lord for His healing touch.

Infection and Healing

Nine-month-old Brandon was a busy baby, busy discovering the world he was growing up in. He crawled from one room to another, picking up anything in his path and putting it in his mouth.

One morning his mama found white pockets of infection in his mouth. He lost his appetite, and it became evident that a trip to the doctor was in order. The doctor prescribed a purple tincture to be painted on the inside of the mouth. As long as the mouth was covered with this purple tincture, it was impossible to see the infection. After using the medication for about five days, the mother decided not to use it one morning so that she could see if Brandon's mouth was healing that evening.

It was with much sadness and regret she saw the inside of his mouth seemed to be even worse. She shared this with Brandon's daddy, and together they decided to seek healing from God. So with a prayer of thanksgiving and trust, they committed their baby to God, asking the Great Physician to heal their baby's mouth.

In the morning, it was with some anxiety that Brandon's mother looked in his mouth. It was clear! There was not a spot of infection. With overflowing hearts, they knelt to thank God for answering their prayer.

Household Hints

When our daughter was eleven and needed to take over more and more household chores, her grandmother gave her a book of household hints. She enjoyed reading this book so much that I wondered just what was holding her attention. Before long, I was reading it, too. I know that we as homemakers enjoy sharing household hints with one another.

Once while reading, I read a hint from another age: "When drawing water and filling a bucket to overflowing, put a piece of wood in it to keep the water steady, and it will not splash out."

In our lives when we feel anxious, worried, or like we could "splash out," we need to put the cross in the middle of our hearts to keep us steady. Psalm 46:10: "Be still, and know that I am God..."

When our loved ones see us enjoying the Word of God and others can see spiritual things holding our attention, it may give them a longing for a spiritual life as well. We should have a joy and peace in our Christian lives that others will take note of and long for the same in their lives.

Hell

Those who belong to the devil will live with him in hell eternally. He wants to possess all so he can take them to hell with him. "The wicked shall be turned into hell, and all the nations that forget God" (Ps. 9:17).

Once there, they will live in fear and terror. There a suffocating heat will envelope them and will cause an unquenchable thirst. "Where their worm dieth not, and the fire is not quenched" (Mark 9:44).

Not only will there be a thirst for cool, clear water but the biggest thirst will be for the love of God. There will be no love or friendship.

The evil one, who possesses one now, will be eternally in control. He will be a harder taskmaster in hell, driving one beyond endurance, but even then there will be no let up. He will inflict extreme thirst, and one will feel tremendous hunger, guilt, unrelenting pain and tiredness. The stench of hell will be all-consuming, but yet there will be no release from it , nor a break from any of its terrors.

The sin we allow in our hearts will poison us, drying up our hearts and sending us to eternal destruction. We need to repent of our sin, turn our backs on it, and confess it. "Therefore also now, saith the Lord, turn ye even to me with all your heart, and with fasting, and with weeping, and with mourning: And rend your heart, and not your garments, and turn unto the Lord your God: for he is gracious and merciful, slow to anger, and of great kindness, and repenteth him of the evil" (Joel 2:12,13).

When our life is cleansed, we need to invite Jesus to come in, and He will give us sweet peace, and Heaven will be our home. "If we confess our sins, he is faithful and just to forgive us our sins, and to cleanse us from all unrighteousness" (1 John 1:9).

Sharing through the Christian Hymnal

"Tell Me the Story of Jesus" for it is "Wonderful Words of Life" and brings "Joy to the World" as "To Us a Child of Hope Is Born." "While Shepherds Watched Their Flocks," "Angels from the Realms of Glory" sang "Glory to God in the Highest." It was a "Silent Night, Holy Night"; it was "Zion's Glad Morning."

"I Have Something I Would Tell You." It is with "Amazing Grace" that "Christ Receiveth Sinful Men." It is with "Love Divine, All Love Excelling," and "Not What These Hands Have Done" but "What Tender Mercy" that "He Loves Me."

"Will the Circle Be Unbroken"? "Have You Any Room for Jesus?" Oh, "Listen to the Gentle Promptings" of the "Holy Spirit, Faithful Guide." He is "Knocking at the Door." Please, "Let Jesus Come into Your Heart," so you can say, "Lord, I'm Coming Home," and you can "Meet Me There."

"Be Ye Strong in the Lord," for "Faith Is a Living Power from Heaven." In fact, "Faith Is the Victory"! So "Let Our Lives and Lips Express" that "The Love of God" is a "Wondrous Love." "It was "Love Found Me."

"Follow the Path of Jesus," and "Be Not Afraid" to "Stand Up, Stand Up for Jesus." "Lean on His Arms" and "Keep Stepping in the Light." "Don't Forget to Pray," and "Cling to the Bible" as you read of "The Unsearchable Riches of Christ." Also "Sing about Jesus," and you will be "Purer in Heart" and have "Heavenly Sunlight."

After a "Sweet Hour of Prayer" at "The Hallowed Spot," "The Golden Gate of Prayer," "My Heart Says Amen" to His will, and I have "Glorious Peace," for "A Full Surrender" brings "Praise to God, Immortal Praise." Now I will be "Standing on the Promises of God," and I will "Yield Not to Temptation" but will "Praise God from Whom All Blessings Flow."

"Tell What He's Done for You," for "Sweet Is the Story." Oh, "Christian, Walk Carefully," for "Dark and Thorny Is the Desert." "Dare to be a Daniel" for "Somebody Follows You." Therefore always "Follow the Path of Jesus."

To "Rescue the Perishing," tell "What a Friend We Have in Jesus." Tell them that "Jesus Saves" and is "A Ransom for All." Then "Tell What He's Done for You," telling them "Grace Is Greater than Our Sin," that "Mercy's Free," and that they need not be "Lost Forever" but to "Look to the Lamb of God," for "Christ Receiveth Sinful Men," because "Jesus Paid It All." We can be "Loyal and True and Faithful."

"I Love to Steal Awhile Away," because "I Love to Think of My Home Above," as "Heaven Holds All to Me." There I will be "Face to Face with Christ," "Safe in the Arms of Jesus," and have "Sweet Rest in Heaven." "There'll Be No Shadows in Heaven" for it will be "The Unclouded Day," and "We'll Never Say Good-by," because we will be "Where the Gates Swing Outward Never."

Oh, may I "Be Ready when He Comes," so I will be found "At the Saviour's Right Hand " and can enter "That Heavenly Home," "The Haven of Rest," where I will sing, "Holy, Holy, Holy," and shout, "All Hail the Power of Jesus' Name," and, "What a Mighty God We Serve."

This is "My Testimony" that He is "The Best Friend of All," "The Lily of the Valley," my "Shelter in the Time of Storm" and the "Rock of Ages, Cleft for Me." "He Was Nailed to the Cross for Me," because "He Loves Me." "Oh, Happy Day" "When Love Lifted Me" "At Calvary." Now "Where Jesus Is, 'Tis Heaven," and I have "Sweet Peace, the Gift of God's Love" for I am "Redeemed—How I Love to Proclaim It."

Scars but Strength

In our country as you are driving along, sometimes in passing a truck, a stone will be thrown at your windshield, causing a bull's-eye, star, or crack. It is possible to repair the damage so that the crack will not continue. First, whatever air is in the crack must be removed. Then a small amount of resin is carefully injected until it fills the crack. Even though the scars of the damage are still seen, it is stronger than it was before the damage happened.

In applying this to our Christian lives, even though sin was the master, we can be forgiven and redeemed. We need to repent, confess, and be washed by the blood of Jesus so the Holy Spirit can apply His love (the material to repair the damage). "That their hearts might be comforted, being knit together in love..." (Col. 2:2). We are now forgiven and redeemed.

Though forgiven and redeemed, we may have scars (memories). Because of God's love, we may be stronger in the areas that were our weaknesses.

Fireplaces, Quilts, and Love

My mother-in-law enjoys quilting, and one of my favorite patterns is the log cabin quilt with the small, red block in the center of the log cabin. The small red block typifies the fireplace in the log cabin.

In one of the quilts she has made, there is a small bit of red showing in each piece; to me this signifies warmth radiating into all the corners. This is how a Christian's life should be, with love in the center radiating to all those around us.

Years ago, when we were newlyweds, John's family went to a national forest in Pennsylvania and rented a cabin with a fireplace. Since John comes from a family of nine children, there was a lot of noise and activity going on around us. It was a time of love and joy.

After three days together, we parted ways, the rest of the family going home and John and I staying for two days longer. The cabin seemed so lonely and cold without the others. That evening I watched with appreciation as John started a fire in the fireplace. Soon the cabin was glowing with light, warmth, and cheerfulness as the fire pushed back the dark and cold.

When God's love has transformed our lives, we need to let it work in and through us, radiating to those around us. His compassion and love are the only weapons a Christian has against the dark, cold world around us.

"And now abideth faith, hope, charity, these three; but the greatest of these is charity" (1 Cor. 13:13).

Empty Chairs

We had five chairs around our family table. One day one was empty, because our son had left home. Seeing the empty chair would cause a lump in my throat. I would often be overtaken with worries and concerns for him.

The Lord spoke to me one day, saying He could fill the chair for me if I would just ask Him to be my guest each day. What a comfort to know He was there each day to comfort me. "...though he be not far from every one of us; For in him we live, and move, and have our being..." (Acts 17:27,28). "...there is a friend that sticketh closer than a brother" (Prov. 18:24).

Whether one loses a family member in death or because of other reasons, I know one would find comfort in inviting Jesus to fill the empty chair. "And I will pray the Father, and he shall give you another Comforter, that he may abide with you forever" (John 14:16).

How about the times we ignore our Savior, leaving an empty chair in His presence? May we be aware of Him in our lives, ever being keen to His presence and voice.

Tangles and Knots

Years ago when we lived in Arizona and the boys were ages five and ten, we would go to the mountains and fish in the lakes and streams. While casting their lines in, the boys would sometimes get tangles in them. Often they would need to ask their father for assistance in getting the tangles out.

Those who quilt or crochet know that sometimes one can get a tangle or knot in the thread or yarn and that it takes carefulness and patience to get the tangle out. What about the times a mother washes her little daughter's hair, and it tangles? A mother knows that if she applies a conditioner, it greatly reduces the tangles.

Sometimes our Christian life gets tangles in it, too. Then we need to give our life to our heavenly Father, asking Him to take control and untangle the mess we have gotten into. With carefulness and patience and by applying God's love, there is a solution to our knots and tangles.

"God is our refuge and strength, a very present help in trouble" (Ps. 46:1).

Cooking and Substitutions

Sometimes a cook may not have all the ingredients for a recipe, and she may substitute something else. If the item she is preparing does not turn out right, there can be disappointments and regrets. One may think, "But it was such a small change. It doesn't seem like it should have made so much difference."

I am thinking about our Christian lives. Suppose we substitute jealousy for rejoicing with our neighbor. It may be such a small amount, we do not think too much of it, but we did allow a little. The next time we might have a bit more jealousy. In no time, our love is not so warm, and we may wonder what is wrong that we do not love our neighbor as we should. The leavening of jealousy continues to grow and soon includes others.

Oh, the regrets we will someday have that we allowed a little leavening of jealousy in our life. If we do stop to look back and consider our spirits and attitudes, we may be surprised that such a "small amount" of jealousy caused so many heartaches and struggles.

I am thinking of another substitution. Suppose your child wants a dog, but you just give him a picture of a puppy. He may like the picture and admire it, but how much more enthusiastic his response would be to a real puppy.

This is how it is when we "know God" instead of "knowing about God." To know God is to have a warm, personal relationship with Him. To only know about Him is to hold Him at arm's length, to like what we see, but it is only a cold, intellectual knowledge.

May we demonstrate our love for God in service to our fellowman. "Thou shalt love the Lord thy God with all thy heart, and with all thy soul, and with all thy strength, and with all thy mind; and thy neighbour as thyself" (Luke 10:27).

Flavorings and the Lord

Have you ever eaten a pizza with ham and pineapple for toppings? At first, it may not sound enticing, but you will find the pineapple enhances the ham, creating a subtle zest and flavor.

Our son likes to make an orange julius to drink occasionally. If he leaves out the vanilla, it loses some of its appeal. The vanilla gives enough flavoring to make it appetizing. There are many foods that need enhancers (flavorings) to bring out their best qualities.

The same is true for us. At first, we may look at a Christ-centered life as not a very enticing life. We need the Lord in our lives, though, to bring out the best in us. He not only brings out our best, He also makes everything turn out right. He can turn a stormy day into one of calmness, a lonely day into one of cheer and joy. He can turn darkness into brightness and a disgruntled soul into a thankful heart. He will turn anger into love, and when we seem to be going backward, He can turn us around, helping us to go forward.

The secret is to invite Him into our hearts and lives and allow Him to work in our lives, bringing out our best and His goodness.

Visiting Friends and the Visitor

I was anxiously awaiting my friends' arrival. But was my house clean enough? Would it pass their inspection? Oh, no, there were some books and magazines lying about, and that looked sloppy. And what about that small water pitcher I used each day for my houseplants? How about my slippers by the side of the bed? There were so many things to pick up and so little time.

Oh, well, no one would ever know. Just open doors and shove things out of sight. What they did not know would not hurt; what would it matter? I did want my friends to feel at home, to be comfortable.

Then on another day, I heard a different kind of knock. I pushed the curtain on my heart's door aside and saw the Lord standing at the door. With dismay, I saw some things I knew He would not be pleased with. If I could quickly better myself and make things look clean. So I tried my old trick, opening doors and hiding things before inviting Him in. Surely He would never know.

He continued knocking, so I opened the door and let Him in. I could feel His tender love and compassion. I saw Him look around my heart; then He went to a closed door, and I thought, "Please, Lord, don't open that door."

But He did. The look He gave me was indescribably tender. He said, "Daughter, let Me apply My cleaning solution, My blood, to your heart. If you will allow Me to clean your dirty house, I will come in and sup with you."

"O Lord, do just that," I cry. "Furthermore, move into my heart, being my permanent companion, for I need Thee every hour."

"Behold, I stand at the door, and knock: if any man hear my voice, and open the door, I will come in to him, and will sup with him, and he with me" (Rev. 3:20).

Trees and Yard Care

To keep a beautiful yard and garden requires much work, carefulness, and diligence. Besides mowing the grass and trimming the bushes, one "weed eats" along sidewalks, around bushes, trees, and buildings.

When weed eating around a gnarled old tree, a person does not need to be as careful as when weed eating around a young tree. The bark on a young tree is tender, and if it is cut through, it might kill the tree. The bark on an old tree is tough and the weed eater string does not cut through it as easily.

Let us make a comparison to Christian life. Young Christians are like young trees. They are tender and sensitive to their surroundings. Were they to receive harsh or critical admonitions, it could destroy them. Whereas an older Christian, likened to an older, established tree, would sooner be able to withstand harshness and a critical attitude.

A Christian, whether young or old, needs to endure the onslaughts of the evil one. But we need to exercise carefulness and tenderness with the young Christian.

"Thou therefore endure hardness, as a good soldier of Jesus Christ" (2 Tim. 2:3). "Blessed is the man that endureth temptations: for when he is tried, he shall receive the crown of life, which the Lord hath promised to them that love him" (James 1:12).

Home Sweet Home

We have a covered patio on the back of our house. The floor is made from boards nailed one to another as closely as possible, but there is a small crack between each one. There are forty-three boards in all; so you know there are a lot of crevices.

One day while sitting on the patio, I noticed a wasp flying about and going between some boards. I decided to mark the place he always flew to, and, sure enough, he would fly to the same crack, going between the boards and staying there, sometimes for quite some time. I knew then that he had his home down there. I marveled how he could tell which boards to fly between. How could he tell where to go? He would leave his home and go about his business, then come back to the same spot, always flying straight and true.

I compare this to our lives. Do we go about our daily business keeping our sights on our heavenly home? Do we stay on the straight and true path going home? Not only did the wasp fly towards home, but he would find himself at home.

So with us if we stay focused and determined, with one goal in mind, we will find ourselves at home.

Riches and Wealth

Marlin and Lynetta have four children. Marlin works hard to make a living, and sometimes he feels discouraged. He feels inadequate, because, financially, he is not as successful as some others.

One day Lynetta, wanting to encourage Marlin, got out her Bible. She wanted to read what the Bible has to say about riches. What are riches, and how necessary are they to one's well-being? Before long she could see that she would need a pencil and paper to write down all she was finding.

"Better is little with the fear of the Lord than great treasure and trouble therewith" (Prov. 15:16).

"Wealth gotten by vanity shall be diminished: but he that gathereth by labour shall increase" (Prov. 13:11).

"Both riches and honour come of thee, and thou reignest over all..." (1 Chron. 29:12).

"...but the substance of a diligent man is precious" (Prov. 12:27).

"A good name is rather to be chosen than great riches, and loving favour rather than silver and gold" (Prov. 22:1).

Lynetta could see there were more, ever so many more, verses on riches and wealth, but it was time to see what the Lord had to say.

"And the cares of this world, and the deceitfulness of riches, and the lusts of other things entering in, choke the word, and it becometh unfruitful" (Mark 4:19).

"Children, how hard is it for them that trust in riches to enter into the kingdom of God! It is easier for a camel to go through the eye of a needle, than for a rich man to enter into the kingdom of God" (Mark 10:24,25).

"But they that will be rich fall into temptation and a snare, and into many foolish and hurtful lusts, which drown men in destruction and perdition. For the love of money is the root of all evil: which while some coveted after, they have erred from the faith, and pierced themselves through with many sorrows. Charge them that are rich in this world, that they be not highminded, nor trust in uncertain riches, but in the living God, who giveth us richly all things to enjoy" (1 Tim. 6:9,10,17).

Lynetta looked about their home. It was comfortably furnished. Indeed, God had been good to them for they were well provided for. It brought to mind one more scripture, "And having food and raiment let us be therewith content" (1 Tim. 6:8). In pondering these verses, Lynetta shuddered to think that with more riches they could lose their souls to destruction, erring from the faith, or they might become highminded and proud.

Lynetta turned to her Bible again. This time she read, "The rich and poor meet together: the Lord is the maker of them all" (Prov. 22:2). She knew that all people everywhere are on common ground; no one is superior because he is more well-to-do. She continued reading, "By humility and the fear of the Lord are riches, and honour, and life."

Then she read, "Who can find a virtuous woman? For her price is far above rubies" (Prov. 31:10). Lynetta's mind was opened to God's real riches. If she would clothe herself with humility and the fear of the Lord and practice the virtues of a Christian wife, she would be an encouragement to Marlin—she could be an asset to Marlin.

Helplessness and Faith

"Suffer the little children to come unto me, and forbid them not: for of such is the kingdom of God" (Mark 10:14).

The quality of childlikeness I wish to talk about is the dependence a child has on his parents or caregiver. A young infant is helpless and has complete faith and trust that his caregiver will care for his needs. The child's love grows for his parents because of helplessness, trust, and faith. I believe this is the confidence we need to give the Lord. We need to feel our helplessness and dependence on Him. With faith, trusting Him to care for our every need, our love for Him grows.

When a mother sees her infant's helplessness and dependence on her, it causes a compassion and love for her child, and a deep bond grows. She is willing, night or day, to exercise her powers to alleviate any distress her child may have. So, also, is God touched with compassion and love when He sees our helplessness and dependence on Him. He is willing, nay, longs, to satisfy our needs. "But thou, O Lord, art a God full of compassion, and gracious, longsuffering, and plenteous in mercy and truth" (Ps. 86:15).

One Road

Recently we were on a trip to another state. On our way home, we drove through a large metropolis where we needed to change roads. We were careful to watch the road signs so we would make the right choice. The sign said to travel in the left lane for our turn-off. That was most unusual as generally one merges to the right when changing to another road. So we especially needed careful concentration and diligence, with faith that this was right. We were careful to stay in the left-hand lane. As we got nearer to our turn-off, we could see that we were wise in obeying the signs. The left lane led to our destination. The middle lane, the one we had been on, led to another route, and the right lane led completely to a different direction. Later, we again were thankful we had carefully followed the signs when we needed to make yet another turn to make the proper connection.

There is a comparison to our Christian lives. We occasionally arrive at a crossroads and need to make a decision. With care and diligence in following the "road signs," we will be able to make the right choice. "I am the Lord thy God...which leadeth thee..." (Isa. 48:17).

Often times the road sign will direct us to take the less traveled road, not the one "everyone else" is traveling. "...leaving us an example, that ye should follow his steps" (1 Pet. 2:21). There may be times when we need to ask which is the right way to take or just inquire if we are traveling the right direction. "But he knoweth the way that I take..." (Job 23:10).

Gardens and Christian Life

Some of us have a garden, and it is important to us. We tend our garden well, watering and fertilizing the plants, pulling weeds, picking up stones, replanting when necessary, and doing whatever else is necessary to maintain a beautiful garden.

In our hearts, we all have a garden. It is our responsibility to maintain this garden. It is, or should be, important to us to keep it beautiful for the Master Gardener. We water and feed the plants, praying and reading the Bible and other good literature. Pulling weeds, removing bad attitudes; picking up stones, repenting of all sins; replanting when necessary, accepting reproof; in general, keeping our love intact.

In the South, it is common to raise catfish for a living. Once as the excavator was digging for a pond, he encountered an immovable object. He was puzzled as he was in an open area. What could possibly be underground that was such an obstruction? With patience and persistence, an old pickup truck was uncovered. It needed to be removed so the catfish pond could be completed.

Suppose we have a corner in our heart where we buried something we held dear or a grievance. It will need to be removed so there will be a place for God's love. With meticulous care and patience, the Master Gardener removes the foreign object. Into the cavity, He will pour His marvelous love. "And the parched ground shall become a pool, and the thirsty land springs of water..." (Isa. 35:7).

The Password

Ten-year-old Ellen liked to play password. True, she was not as good as her two older brothers, but it was a challenge. The word she needed to describe was *metropolis,* which she knew was a large city. Speaking of large cities, she, being a Kansas country girl, had never seen a really large city, for sure not one she could call a metropolis. She would soon, though, as they were going to California for Christmas to see her aunt and uncle. Dad had already told her they were going to go through Albuquerque, and that was a large city.

A week before Christmas the family was on their way to California. Who would she play with? Her cousin was just a small baby girl. When they arrived at their uncle's home, it was fun to hold wee baby Sherry and listen to the grown-ups talk. She liked a wall motto on Aunt Neoma's living room wall. It was just like a mirror, only it was blue. She had never seen one like it before. Then she read the words, "The gift of God is eternal life through Jesus Christ our Lord" (Rom. 6:23). Immediately she pictured a large wrapped gift with a pretty bow on it.

At twelve years of age, Ellen asked Jesus to forgive her sins and to come into her heart. A few months later they visited her aunt and uncle again. She looked to see whether the wall motto was still there on the living room wall, and it was! Now she understood it better. God had given Jesus to die for her sins so that someday she could live in Heaven.

Time hurried on. Soon Ellen was in her youth years where one of the delights was singing. She enjoyed singing and learning new songs. Years later she heard a song that had this phrase in it, "When they ask me how I made it, quickly I'll say it, 'By the blood of the Lamb, I made it through.'"

Not long after when some friends were at Ellen and her husband's house, they were discussing a sermon they had heard. It was about the Gileadites and their enemies, but it was hard to tell who was foe or friend. They knew there was one word the foe could not pronounce correctly, and that was "Shibboleth." If the word was pronounced "Sibboleth," then they knew it was an enemy and they would do away with him (Judg. 12:6). The thought was advanced how when we arrive at Heaven's gate, we will need to know the correct password to enter in. We will not only say it, it will be written on our forehead. "And I looked, and, lo, a Lamb stood on the mount Sion, and with him an hundred forty and four thousand, having his Father's name written in their foreheads" (Rev. 14:1).

Ellen thought over the years and remembered the wall motto in her uncle's house. She was so thankful God had given her the gift of eternal life, that she could say, "By the blood of the Lamb, I have made it through." She was thankful to have the password written on her forehead.

The Lighthouse and My Boat

My little boat was cast out to sea. It was fun to be in command of my boat as the sea was smooth and glassy. I could not imagine a storm; the sun was shining and there was a gentle breeze. Ah, but life was good.

Before I traveled too far, though, I noticed a subtle change in the sky, and had the breeze picked up just a little? I chose to ignore any change—life was so good, and I was having such fun.

Then one afternoon I knew without a doubt there was a storm brewing. I could not ignore the storm warnings any longer. How had this happened to me? I did not deserve such as this; I had never done anything very bad. The sky got darker, and the storm picked up its speed. Oh, how it battered my boat! I was really tossed about, and the waves almost covered me.

Night was falling, and soon it was dark all around me. Where could I go? Was that a faint glimmer of Light ahead of me? I set my sights on the Light. That was my goal. It was a long terrifying night. It seemed I was tossed to and fro and that I did not get closer to the Light. Once the wind died down, and I thought I heard a Voice call my name. Then the wind whipped up more vehemently. I was terrified. I could not help myself. "Jesus," I called, "save me before I perish."

Then I saw a small boat coming toward me. Was it friend or foe? I heard the Pilot of the small boat say, "Follow Me, and I'll guide you to the lighthouse."

Oh, a lighthouse! How thankful I was to know there was safety ahead, but I could not control my boat. Then I realized the other Pilot was aware of my condition, because He threw out a lifeline to me. I grabbed a hold of it and hung on. It felt so good to be doing something for my safety.

Finally we were at the lighthouse, and I heard the Voice call my name again. I knew it was time to relinquish my hold on my security, but could I trust in another? I was in indecision, willing and yet unwilling. Then I heard the Voice say, "Come unto me, all ye that labour and are heavy laden, and I will give you rest" (Matt. 11:28). Ah, that was what I wanted. That was what I yearned for.

I asked Jesus to come into my boat and be my Pilot. Now I do not need to fear the wind and storms. When it seems there are swelling tides about me, Jesus commands the waves, "Peace, be still." I know that if Jesus is my Pilot, He will land me safe on yonder shore. Hallelujah!

Onions, Leeks, and Garlic

"We remember the fish, which we did eat in Egypt freely; the cucumbers, and the melons, and the leeks, and the onions, and the garlick" (Num. 11:5).

Carolee was having her husband's family over for Friday evening supper and needed groceries. She had decided to have lasagna, taco salad, garlic toast, and melons, since melons were in season.

As Carolee was shopping for vegetables and fruits, she was wondering what to have for dessert. When she saw the apples, she thought of apple cake with warm butter sauce. Perfect. Feeling quite pleased with herself, she put a bag of apples into her cart.

Friday morning arrived, but before Carolee began her day of cooking, she picked up her Bible to read. She had begun at the beginning of the Bible and was now ready for Numbers 11.

Later when Carolee was preparing the food for her guests she was thinking about what she had read. It was interesting that she was using the foods mentioned in verse 5 for her supper. How bland lasagna would be without onions or garlic. Carolee continued thinking about the Israelites. She could understand how old it would get to have only one kind of food to eat, but to go back to the captivity of Egypt for onions, garlic, and leeks? Surely not. Who would go back to captivity for that?

But, wait a minute, what about Christian life? How many times did one think the Bible was boring and there were more exciting books to read? What about the desire to be fashionable? What about having the best in our homes or on our farms? If one's thoughts centered on self and the cares of life, was not this grabbing an onion or perhaps some garlic? Wouldn't it be sad to be near the journey's end and turn around for an onion or garlic? Of course, if one knew they were near journey's end, they surely would not turn around, but most of us do not know when our end will be.

"Therefore be ye also ready: for in such an hour as ye think not the Son of man cometh" (Matt. 24:44).

The Old Path

"Thus saith the Lord, Stand ye in the ways, and see, and ask for the old paths, where is the good way, and walk therein, and ye shall find rest for your souls" (Jer. 6:16).

Rebekah was weary of the long journey. Would it never end? Traveling on the Oregon Trail had been fun and interesting for awhile, but now it was the same scenery day after day. She was tired of bumping along, sometimes in ruts so deep the wagons almost hung up in them. But Rebekah was glad they were not the first ones going west—others had gone before, and the trail was clearly marked. She thought with longing of the smoother roads back home.

One day they saw a rocking chair by the trail. Ma said someone had needed to lighten their load. Rebekah glanced around her, wondering what they could leave behind if that should happen to them.

A few days later, Pa said they were climbing higher, but you could not tell it. Rebekah went to the back of the covered wagon to look out. Sure enough, they were climbing. But when you looked out the front you saw nothing different to tell that you were climbing, only the same old path.

Then one day Pa said the horses were tiring and the load was too heavy for them. He asked Ma if they had anything extra. Ma answered quickly, "David, you know we have nothing extra." Pa gave his shoulders a slight shrug and turned away. Later he asked Ma if she had thought of anything they could discard. She answered that if it was truly necessary, they could take the bedding out of the wooden trunk Grandpa had given her, and the trunk could be left behind. She added, and her lips quivered, "You know it is special to me; it is the trunk Grandma brought across from the old country."

Pa put his arm around Ma and said, "Elizabeth, I'm sorry. Is the price of having our own place too high? Would you rather we turn around? "Ma squared her shoulders and went to her precious wooden trunk and emptied it. Then she told Pa he could do with it as he felt best.

At long last, Pa said they were nearing the trail's end. They were happy and very thankful to be near the end of the journey.

Years later Rebekah told her grandchildren about their journey on the Oregon Trail. She told the children that many others had gone before them. Others had marked the trail so clearly and well that their journey had been easier and safer because of what the earlier travelers had done.

Are we sometimes weary of the long journey from here to our heavenly home? Do we think back with wistfulness to the smooth trail we left behind to climb the rugged path upward? Are we at times critical of others, wondering at their unnecessary baggage? Do we feel that the way is too narrow and that there are some old ways others are hung up on? Is the price higher than I am willing to pay? Last, but not least, are we pointing our children to the old path, telling them the path is a good way and teaching them to walk therein?

May we, with thankfulness and jubilation, look forward to our journey's end where we shall find rest, sweet rest, for our souls.

Connection to God

We have a cordless telephone. It is very handy and allows one to make contact with family and friends easily. When we lived in a large metropolitan area and there were a lot of cordless telephones on our street, it was common for the handset to lose its identity to its base. To have the handset gain back its identity to its base, one had to put the handset back onto its base. Sometime if one snatched up the handset too quickly, the connection between the base and handset would again be lost.

A Christian has a "cordless telephone" to Heaven. He can contact God at any time. Occasionally a Christian can become so busy and involved with the activities of the day that he loses contact with his Creator. Then he needs to come back to God, his Base, centering on Him so he can regain his identity with God. If he has a quick prayer and is off to his pursuits again, he may find that he really is not in touch with his Father.

"But it is good for me to draw near to God..." (Ps.73:28). "Pray without ceasing" (1 Thess. 5:17).

Treasures of Our Homes

Glenda had invited some of her friends for brunch. It seemed like it had been a long time since the friends had been together. She told the mothers to bring their toddlers and babies. She had counted up the children and knew there would be quite a lot of them. Oh, well, it would be a good time for all, even though there would be a lot of noise, and the older children would help care for the little ones.

On the day of the brunch, the house was full and running over with children and mothers. The twelve-year-old twins, Jayda and Jayla, felt like they had it made! So many babies to hold and play with. It was a relief, though, when their friend, Jaylene, joined them.

The thirteen mothers sat around the dining room table, and it was natural for the conversation to center around children. They were sharing their experiences on training their children when they decided to go around the table and each mother would share an encouragement or an admonition that she felt. They wanted to consider what the others said and to take it as if it were said to each one personally.

Since it was Glenda's home and she was sitting at the head of the table, she would start. "I feel each child should be taught to obey immediately. If on disobedience a child is met with sure discipline, he would learn to obey promptly. 'Children, obey your parents in the Lord: for this is right' " (Eph. 6:1).

Joyce, who sat next to Glenda, said, "A child should be taught to respect. First of all, they need to respect daddy and mommy and then grandparents and older folks. If a child is taught to obey and respect, he will have obedience and respect for all authority. 'Honour thy father and mother; which is the first commandment with promise' " (Eph. 6:2).

"Speaking of respect," Shirley said, "we need to teach babies and young children to respect their older siblings' belongings and vice versa. It is never right for a child to open their siblings' drawers and look through them."

"Let's continue this chain of thought," spoke Vivian. "A child must be taught that other people's property needs to be respected. Children should not open anyone's cupboards, drawers, or refrigerators. That includes Grandma's, too."

Teresa was next. "Talking of respect, one cannot forget respect for God's house. 'I was glad when they said unto me, Let us go into the house of the Lord' " (Ps. 122:1). She felt that a young baby should be taught that quietness was of importance when the Word of God was read at home or church. Teresa said, "Quietness needs to be taught during prayer, also."

Elizabeth said that jealousy was common in people and should be watched for among our children. She quoted Song of Solomon 8:6: " '...jealousy is cruel as the grave: the coals thereof are coals of fire, which hath a most vehement flame.' Let's not forget to teach our children to be kind to one another, to animals, and to those less fortunate."

Sondra wondered what else could be said. "We need to take time out of our schedules to read, hold, or play with our children. We will have them on our knees and at our elbows only once. Be lavish with your love and affection. 'That their hearts might be comforted, being knit together in love...' "(Col. 2:2).

Julie said that as a child she had had many fears, and it was always a comfort when Dad had family devotions and prayed for God's protection to be over them. She recalled hearing Dad read the Bible storybook and other good books. She said that in the mornings if her dad was gone to work, her mother would read from the Bible and pray with them. There were some days she and her siblings just could not get along. At those times, Mother would call them all to her side and have them kneel in a circle. Mother then would pray, asking God to renew their love for one another. "And the Lord make you to increase and abound in love one toward another, and toward all men..." (1 Thess. 3:12).

Mary said that teaching a child honesty and truthfulness is very important as it is a human tendency to tell a lie to save face. "Thou shalt not bear false witness against thy neighbour" (Exod. 20:16).

Regina reminded everyone to discipline with firmness but in charity. She also said that after a child has been disciplined, he should be cuddled or loved to let him know he is not disliked but loved and that you hold nothing against him.

Starla said that with all these admonitions, mothers need to begin each day with God. First with prayer, telling God our struggles, asking Him for His help. We should tell Him our joys and pray for each family member. She reminded each one to read a portion of God's Word, saying that it would help us in our thought life. "I have set the Lord always before me..." (Ps. 16:8).

Next Rita spoke, "I feel like I really should not speak since I have a child who is wayward, and I know I have made many mistakes. But I want to encourage you all to be faithful, for we have Heaven to gain and hell to shun. The only possessions we can take to Heaven are our children. I want to encourage you to, first of all, love your children's father, showing him submission and respect. Your children will see that and learn respect, love, and obedience to him."

Phyllis had this concluding thought, "We should not hesitate to confess our faults to our children. It will cause their confidence in us to grow. Always end each day with God, asking Him for His forgiveness for wrongs committed, then trust in His atoning blood. '...the blood of Jesus Christ his Son cleanseth us from all sin'" (1 John 1:7).

Heaven, Our Home

What can be more inviting than to think of our heavenly home, the wonder and joy of it all? We have heard of the eight wonders of the world; so also there are eight wonders of Heaven, yea, even nine wonders.

1. The first wonder is that there is such a place as Heaven. We know there is such a place, for Jesus said, "In my Father's house are many mansions: if it were not so, I would have told you. I go to prepare a place for you" (John 14:2). The overwhelming beauty and splendor of God, His glory, will fill all of Heaven. We will stand in awe and amazement at the rapture and beauty, at the glory of God.

2. The wonder of such a holy place, that there is no sin there. "And there shall in no wise enter into it any thing that defileth, neither whatsoever worketh abomination, or maketh a lie: but they which are written in the Lamb's book of life" (Rev. 21:27).

3. The wonder of the inhabitants. There are angels in Heaven who help us. "Are they not all ministering spirits [angels], sent forth to minister for them who shall be heirs of salvation"(Heb. 1:14)? "Likewise, I say to you, there is joy in the presence of the angels of God over one sinner that repenteth: (Luke 15:10). "Bless the Lord, ye his angels, that excel in strength, that do his commandments, hearkening unto the voice of his word" (Ps. 103:20). There are many references in the Bible to angels and other inhabitants, too. "Then I looked, and I heard the voice of many angels around the throne, the living creatures, and the elders; and the number of them was ten thousand times ten thousand, and thousands of thousands" (Rev. 5:11). Also, "All the angels stood around the throne and the elders and the four living creatures, and fell on their faces before the throne of God and worshipped God" (Rev. 7:11).

4. The wonder that He has interest in you and me! "And he said unto me, It is done. I am Alpha and Omega, the beginning and the end. I will give unto him that is athirst of the fountain of the water of life freely. He that

overcometh shall inherit all things; and I will be his God, and he shall be my son" (Rev. 21:6,7). Also, "Blessed are they that do his commandments, that they may have right to the tree of life, and may enter in through the gates into the city" (Rev. 22:14).

5. The wonder of Heaven's perfection and beauty (Rev. 21:16; 22:5). The glory, splendor, and majesty of Heaven are beyond what we can comprehend. Let us contemplate, though, what the Bible has to say. The walls are jasper; the city is pure gold. The foundations are of precious stones, and the gates are of pearl. The streets are of pure gold as transparent glass. There will be no temple, as God and the Lamb are the temple. There will be no need of the sun or moon, as the glory of God lightens it, and the Lamb is the light thereof (Rev. 21;22,23). From the throne of God, the river of life, as clear as crystal, flows. On each side of the river are trees bearing twelve kinds of fruit and a fresh crop each month (Rev. 22:1,2).

The beauty of Heaven cannot be compared to anything on earth. The landscape, flowers, greenery, and vegetation are beyond our description. The music will surround us till we will seem a part of it. And to know that we can share in this splendor!

Nothing will be lacking in Heaven. There will be no guilt, no trials or temptations. There will be deliverance from heartaches, tragedies, disasters, and disappointments. "And God shall wipe away all tears from their eyes; and there shall be no more death, neither sorrow, nor crying, neither shall there be any more pain: for the former things are passed away" (Rev. 21:4). Oh, I want to go there, don't you? There will be no pain, sorrow, or grief. There we will be united with our loved ones, never needing to say good-bye.

6. The sixth wonder of Heaven is that it is so accessible. "On the east three gates; on the north three gates; on the south three gates; and on the west three gates" (Rev. 21:13). The three gates on the east (the sun rises in the east, starting a new day) mean there is access to Heaven for little children. "But Jesus said, Suffer little children, and forbid them not, to come unto me: for of such is the kingdom of heaven" (Matt. 19:14). The three

gates on the west (the sun sets in the west, ending the day) say there is access for the old. The three gates on the north are for the cold or those in sin and trouble. The gates on the south are for those who have wealth or are living in pleasure. There is an open door for all to come to Heaven, an open door for all nationalities. "And before him shall be gathered all nations..." (Matt. 25:32).

7. The seventh wonder is of the conditions it takes to get there. Only those who have repented and been cleansed will be there. "Verily, verily, I say unto thee, Except a man be born again, he cannot see the kingdom of God" (John 3:3). Also Matthew 18:3, "Except ye be converted, and become as little children, ye shall not enter into the kingdom of heaven."

After this, we need to be baptized by the Holy Spirit. "I indeed have baptized you with water: but he shall baptize you with the Holy Ghost" (Mark 1:8).

We must have our first love on Jesus. "O love the Lord, all ye his saints: for the Lord preserveth the faithful..." (Ps. 31:23).

We need obedience to God. "Obey my voice, and I will be your God, and ye shall be my people: and walk ye in all the ways that I have commanded you, that it may be well unto you" (Jer. 7:23).

We need to be humble. "Humble yourselves therefore under the mighty hand of God, that he may exalt you in due time" (1 Pet. 5:6).

Next, we need to be teachable. "Teach me to do thy will..." (Ps. 143:10).

Also we need to be submissive. "O Lord, thou art our father; we are the clay, and thou our potter..." (Isa. 64:8).

8. Wonder number eight is the wonder of Jesus. "Wonderful Jesus! marvelous King! Ever His praise my spirit shall sing, When I behold His glorified face, How I shall praise His wonderful grace!" He is our comforter and joy. "...and, lo, I am with you alway, even unto the end of the world" (Matt. 28:20).

9. The ninth wonder is that more people do not prepare themselves for Heaven.

Children
of All Ages

Giving Flowers

"Oh, Mom, I love you," said five-year-old Melody, throwing her arms around her mother. Slipping into the living room, she picked up the toys and entertained baby Aaron. Her mother, thinking about it later, felt like she had received a bouquet of flowers.

Ten-year-old Timothy crept silently into the dining room and set the table for Mother, knowing she was busy putting up strawberries.

"Dad and Mom, I'm sorry for being disrespectful and disobedient," said thirteen-year-old Shayla. "I will try to do better."

When fifteen-year-old Heather reconsecrated her life to God, she said, "I'm thankful, Mom, that I was chosen to help you in your handicapped condition."

One evening after church, Steve gathered his family together and, clearing his throat, brought a confession to his wife and children, telling them he was sorry for speaking so harshly and being too demanding.

Marie, who had been married two years, lifted her tear-filled eyes and said, "Honey, I'm sorry I wanted to have my way, that I was not submissive to you. Will you forgive me?"

Nineteen-year-old Lance came to Mother's typewriter, thinking he would type a quick note to a friend. Seeing his mother had been typing her grocery list, he quickly typed, "Mom, I love you!"

Going to a nursing home to visit her father, Elaine stopped to speak to Mr. Koehn. He told her he was happy and had the joy of salvation in his heart.

These are all flowers that have been given to loved ones. Gentle words of kindness and deeds of love are flowers along the way.

Are we remembering to give our loved ones flowers?

Christmas and Patience

One Christmas season, six-year-old Grace saw a lovely wrapped gift in her mother's closet. Being of an inquisitive nature, she interrogated her mother on whose it was. Within time she discovered it was hers. She hugged herself with delight. It was fun dreaming about what was in that charmingly wrapped gift. But it didn't stay with just dreaming and anticipation. Before long she was badgering her mother with questions. What could it be? She had so many wants, and Christmas was so far away. It was still two weeks till that special day. Would it ever come?

After a time, Mother decided it was time to teach Miss Impatience a lesson. She gave the gift to Grace and told her she could open it. What joy, but then, somehow it had lost some of its appeal. It wasn't quite as much fun when no one else was opening a gift.

But, oh! It was a lovely set of dishes. Such cute plates, cups, and saucers and dear little forks, spoons, and knives. That wasn't all. There were little pots and pans to cook with, a small waffle iron, and more. Oh, the delight and magical hours of fun.

Then one morning there were so many things to do that there wasn't time to play with dishes. Anyway, it didn't matter, as tomorrow was Christmas.

Before Grace knew it, it was Christmas morning. They were going to Grandpa and Grandma's house, and everything was ready. There were the pies Mother had made for the yummy dinner they would get. And what was more exciting, there were the Christmas gifts they would open later.

Dinner was over, and it was time for surprises. First, though, Grandpa would read the Christmas story, and some Christmas carols would be sung.

The baby of them all had his name called first. Then the next youngest, and so on until it was finally time for Cynthia, who was just before Grace.

How interesting. Cynthia's gift was the same size and wrapped in the same paper as Grace's dishes had been wrapped in.

By the way, where were her dishes? Never mind, there wasn't time to think about it now. She would look for them when she got home.

Cynthia's gift was dishes, the exact same set as Grace had received two weeks ago. They looked so pretty in their special big box.

Now was the grand moment. The time she had been waiting for for so long. Grace's gift was handed to her. What could it be? It was a smaller box than Cynthia's gift had been. She tore off the paper and lifted the lid. She gave a gasp of dismay and disappointment. Here were her dishes, only they were not in a pretty box and arranged enticingly. Rather, they were helter-skelter in a smaller box, and she had played with them before, so it wasn't exciting anymore.

Grace had learned her lesson. Never again did she beg to know what her gifts might be.

Sometime we can hardly wait for the future. We may be tempted to try or "taste" an experience before the time is "just right." Then we will have remorse and bitter tears of regret. Thankfully, God is forgiving, yet the scars, or memories, remain.

Peace and Goodwill

It was a month until Christmas. Ronnie and Alice contemplated what they could do with their six children to promote peace and goodwill.

They decided to draw names. Then they explained to the children that they wanted to teach them what peace and goodwill are. Every day they were to do something special for the person whose name they had drawn. They were to do it in secret, not letting anyone know whose name they had. Then on Christmas eve, they were to give a gift to this person.

Fourteen-year-old Dwight had gotten Anna's name. It would not be hard to choose a gift to give her. After all, a six-year-old had lots of wishes. But to do other kind deeds? Now that would be different. She could be such a pest, always asking so many questions, wanting to see his models, taking his special drawing pencils, and, well, you know, just being a pain.

The first day when Mom called Anna from upstairs to come set the table, it was not hard to jump up and set the table. It was a joy to see her delight when she bounced into the dining room and saw the table already set.

Then there were days when he had to search for kind things to do. And not only that, he needed to do them in secret. He soon discovered the best way to keep his secret was to do kind deeds for his other siblings.

In the meantime, who had his name? Could it be ten-year-old Frank, or his older sister, Julie? It was a pleasure to step into his bedroom after breakfast and find his bed fixed. Surely it was Julie, but then, how about the time he came into the barn and found his chores done?

Soon it was Christmas morning. How time had flown, and how seldom he had heard anyone asking or wishing for gifts. That evening Mom and Dad told everyone they thought the plan to promote peace and goodwill had been a success. They decided to make this a family tradition every year.

Dwight went to bed that evening with a special warm feeling in his heart for his younger sister. He realized that doing all the special things for her had helped him to love her more. God's love for us caused Him to send His only Son to bring peace and goodwill to all.

Christmas

When we were waiting the birth of our children, we were thrilled and excited. We were anxious and could hardly wait for the day to come when the new baby would be here.

There was a Baby whom all the world was looking for, because God had promised that He would send a Savior.

After years of waiting, God sent an angel to Mary, a young girl who was engaged to be married. At first she was frightened, but the angel said, "Fear not, Mary, for thou hast found favour with God...And, behold, thou shalt bring forth a son, and shalt call his name Jesus."

Mary wondered how this was possible, because she was only engaged to Joseph. But the angel said, "With God all things are possible." So the special Baby was on His way.

One day many weeks later there was knock on the door. It was an officer from Caesar Augustus. He said all the world was to be taxed, and they needed to register in their hometown.

Mary and Joseph would need to make a trip, because Joseph was of the house and lineage of David. This was surely the wrong time to take a trip, because soon the special Baby was to be born.

It was a long and tiresome trip for Mary. Finally, they came over a hill and could see Bethlehem. Like any caring husband, Joseph was anxious to find a clean room and bed for Mary. But Joseph was told there was no room at the inn. He told the innkeeper, "But, sir, my wife is expecting a Baby, and I think He will come tonight."

With sympathy, the innkeeper offered his stable, saying, "This is all I have left; at least you will have privacy and be warm and dry." With the clean straw the innkeeper brought, Joseph made a bed for Mary.

That night the Baby was born. They called His name Jesus. He was "wrapped in swaddling clothes and laid in a manger."

Not far away from Bethlehem were some shepherds taking care of their sheep. While watching their sheep the night of Jesus' birth, there appeared to them a bright light in the sky and an angel. They were frightened. But the angel said, "Fear not, for, behold, I bring you good tidings of great joy which shall be for all people. A Savior, the Messiah, has been born in Bethlehem."

Suddenly there was with the angel a host of angels praising God and saying, "Glory to God in the highest and on earth, peace, goodwill toward men!"

When the angels left, the shepherds said, "Let us go and see this wonderful Baby."

Come, go with me to Bethlehem; it is not far away. Let us see our Savior; He is just a prayer away.

Building Character

Dear Daughter,

Now is the time when you are building your character. During your childhood, your parents, teachers, grandparents, and friends have had a lot to do in influencing your character building. Now that you are getting older, a lot of choices will be yours.

Will you choose honesty or deceitfulness, purity in thought and action, humility or pride, love and forgiveness?

If you were to sew a dress, you would, first of all, take out your pattern. So also in your character building, you will need a pattern. The perfect pattern is Jesus. If you will pattern your life after His, you will be happy.

The Christian's most important guide is the Holy Spirit. Our road map is the Bible. Other good reading material will also help, but never let it take the place of the Word of God.

Just as it is important to know God's Word so also we need to talk to Him. We should tell Him everything. He knows all about us, but it shows our trust and confidence in Him when we open our hearts to Him.

To choose right may at times cause a struggle, but in the end it will be worth it—not only in this life will we reap rewards, but in the life to come, there will be an eternal home in Heaven.

May you always choose precious stones for your building.

Love,

Mom

Precious Stones

Dear Daughter,

In the previous letter I wrote, I spoke of building your character. I would like to talk of the precious stones you need to choose to build with. I mentioned some choices you have, but I want to mention them again, as they are very important and cannot be stressed enough.

First of all, choose Jesus to be your foundation. Then choose good reading material to help you build.

Choose friends who are also on their way to Heaven. You want friends who are respectful and sincere. Do not hesitate to choose some "older" friends. They are concerned about your soul and will lend a listening ear and an understanding heart.

I mentioned a friend who has sincerity, but you need to be sincere, too. A sincere person is humble, honest, loving, and cheerful. These are all precious stones for your building.

Another important area to look at is our character in the home. Whatever attributes we want our friends to see and know us by, we need to practice them in the home.

Cheerfulness will lighten your load. Patience and gentleness are some precious stones, too. Some very important building materials are love and forgiveness. It has been said, "Those we love the most, we hurt the most." Let that not be your life. We need to be forgiving and remember, "A soft answer turneth away wrath."

Some more important stones for your building are obedience and submission. If you build with these stones and God gives you a home of your own, building that home will be a happy task.

A precious stone God has asked you to build with is kindness and understanding for a handicapped person. May you use kindness to all you meet.

Remember, always choose Jesus for your best friend. He will never let you down.
                              Love,
                          Mom

Wisdom of Obedience

Once there was a young family with two small boys who lived near a small recreational pond. The pond attracted ducks and geese to live in and around it.

The boys had great delight whenever their mother would give them crumbs of any kind to feed the ducks and geese. Not only was it fun feeding the birds, but it was fun teasing them, too. Often times, Mom would warn them not to antagonize the birds, as they might retaliate.

One day the younger boy forgot, or maybe he rebelled against his mother's wisdom, and he teased an old gander. When he tired of his sport and turned to walk away, the gander came after him and nipped him in the back.

Too late the lad realized, "Mother knows best."

Are we not like this youngster when we rebel or disobey our heavenly Father? Do we remember, "Father knows best"?

A Little Black Sheep

Two-and-one-half-year old James and his mother sat together in the rocking chair. "Sing, Mommy, sing," said the little one.

"What shall I sing?" asked Mommy.

"Sing 'A Little Black Sheep,'" replied James. So, together they sang.

> A little black sheep was playing one day
> In a meadow where wild flowers grow.
> When the sun went down, 'twas then he got lost,
> And he didn't know how to go home.
> He cried and he cried for he had been bad;
> He wished he had never done wrong.
> He thought to himself, "I'm just a black sheep;
> They won't even care that I'm gone."
>
> Chorus:
> Here, sheep. Here, sheep.
> Listen, little sheep, poor little black sheep,
> Someone is calling for you.
> Listen, little sheep, poor little black sheep,
> Someone is searching for you.
>
> The master's big dog found the little black sheep,
> And beside him laid down on the ground.
> He barked and he barked, and he cried and he cried,
> So glad that the lost had been found.
> Sometimes boys and girls, like the little black sheep,
> Get in trouble when they disobey.
> But if they'll always do what they're told to do,
> They'll always be happy and gay. *

By the time the song ended, James was fast asleep. His mother carefully put him into his bed; then she kneeled beside the bed and prayed, "Father, when You are calling and searching for him, help him to hear Your voice.

And in his hour of temptation, be near him and help him to be successful in his Christian life."

When James was five years old, his favorite song was, "Wonderful Story of Love." For the Sunday evening Christmas program, he and his mother sang the song in front of the church. That night she prayed, "Father, help James to always love the wonderful story of love, and when he is called to give his heart to You, or when he is far away, that he will remember and hear Your voice."

At eleven years of age, the Lord tenderly called James. James yielded his heart and life to God. His favorite song was, "Redeemed—How I Love to Proclaim It." The night he spoke his vows to the Lord in front of many witnesses, he sang it with enthusiasm.

Before retiring for the night, with a heart full of thankfulness, James' mother thanked the Lord that her son had answered his first call. She was thankful he chose to unite with God's people. She prayed that he would always love to tell of his redemption, sharing that he was God's child, that he would not be ashamed to tell the wonderful story of love.

Then several years later, James was "in the meadow where wild flowers grow. When the sun went down, 'twas then he got lost, And he didn't know how to go home."

Is he crying and wishing he had never done wrong? Will there be the master's big dog to find him, and beside him on the ground to lie down, willing to stay with him, to tell him the wonderful story of love again? Then he can say, "The lost has been found," and the song again will be, "Redeemed—How I Love to Proclaim It."

Permission sought.

Growing Up

Tyson and his mother went to visit Anna. Anna had a lovely home, and she had many things that interested little boys. One thing Tyson enjoyed was the cuckoo clock. It was with joy and amusement that he watched the little bird come out of the door and cuckoo.

As Tyson ate some chocolate chip cookies and drank a glass of milk, he watched the tiny bird come out of the little door and cuckoo ten times. He watched the chain drop a little lower with each strike. So that was it, that is what made the cuckoo work.

Soon after refreshments, Anna and Mother went out to look at the garden. At first, Tyson had fun playing with Shep, the dog. Then Shep tired and lay down to have a nap. Tyson wandered around the yard, playing on the swing for a time, but it got boring playing by himself.

Mother and Anna were now looking at the flowers. How Tyson longed to go back inside, to be where it was cool. "I know," he thought, "I'll just go back in. I'll lie down like Shep and have a nap."

When he came in the door, he heard the cuckoo give three calls and stop. How disappointing to have it stop so soon. He did not even get to watch it. Then he thought, "I'll just pull on the chain so I can watch it. I don't want to wait till the big hand travels all the way around again. It goes so slow."

So he pulled on the chain, and there was a crash. He had pulled the clock down!

Are we sometimes impatient, longing to grow up before our time or pushing our way through with what we want? We should think it not strange when our world comes crashing down around us if we have been impatient.

The Shining Moon

Thomas, who was in the fourth grade, enjoyed science. His favorite subject was astronomy. He enjoyed learning about the sun, moon, and stars. It was a real pleasure when he could answer his four-year-old sister's questions.

When she asked why the moon was not as bright as the sun, he could tell her that the moon could shine only because it reflected the sun. He explained that were the sun to go out, the moon would not shine either.

Mother heard their conversation and knew this was a good time to do some teaching also. She explained that it is the same in our lives. That if we live close to Jesus, God's Son, then we will reflect Him. He is our light, and we will shine with His light. But when we are far from Him, we will not shine.

Inferiority

Donna braced herself, patting her hair into place, smoothing out her skirt, and glancing into the mirror for the third time to see that all was in place before she would walk into church. But just at that moment, two girls walked in. They were chatting together so amiably that immediately Donna felt left out. Out of the corner of her eye, she watched them. They looked so sure of themselves, every detail of their clothing and hair was just so right. Why could not she be more like them? She would have to lose some more weight, comb her hair a little differently, and make that pattern of dress. Oh, my, she felt sloppy.

Not knowing how Donna was feeling, the girls drifted out of the entry room into the sanctuary of the church.

The next to enter the mirrored area was Donna's Aunt Susie. Aunt Susie had not known why she felt compelled to go into the rest room, but seeing Donna, she felt the Spirit asking her to let Donna know she cared for her. Putting her arms around Donna, Aunt Susie said, "Donna, I love you." This was all Donna needed to open a floodgate of tears and questions.

"Aunt Susie, why can't I be more like other girls? They always seem so sure of themselves; their hair and clothes always seem so, well, just right, and I feel so, so inferior."

"Oh, Donna, if you could only know how much God loves you! Why He made you in His own image. What a glorious thought that our Creator patterned us after Himself. Not only that, He calls us His children. He wants our love and devotion. Walk with joy in your heart, because you are a daughter of the King!"

Donna breathed a small thanksgiving prayer in her heart for Aunt Susie. With shining eyes, she turned and gave her aunt a dazzling smile. It was easy to walk into church and much easier to meet her peers.

Whenever the old fears started nagging her, she would always think these thoughts, "I'm a daughter of the King and created in His image. He does so much for me." Thinking these thoughts, she could love her Creator more.

Tea Parties and Tea Kettles

Sierra is a little girl who enjoys giving tea parties. It is her delight to invite her cousins, Brittany and Katelyn, over for tea. What fun to use an old-fashioned tea kettle that whistles merrily when it comes to a boil. Sometimes the girls watch anxiously for the kettle to come to a boil so they can hear its merry whistle. But how long it takes; how slow it can be!

One day the girls were entertained by Sierra's puppy and did not hear the whistle. They followed the puppy outside. After awhile, Brittany said, "Sierra, we forgot about our tea party." They hurried into the house, but a merry whistle did not greet them. Instead they saw a mess, with water all over Mother's clean stove. After cleaning up, they needed to begin all over. This time they watched the pot.

When one turns the heat down under a tea kettle, you can listen to its merry whistle. But if the heat is not turned down, it will hiss and spew forth its steam till it is empty and dry. So, too, in our cooking, if the soup comes to a boil, we need to turn it down so it will not boil over and make a mess, requiring a major cleanup job. I have heard the adage, "A watched pot never boils."

I am thinking of our lives and how real it is that when we are in a trial, if we watch and pray, or turn the heat down, we will not boil over. "Watch and pray, that ye enter not into temptation" (Matt. 26:41). "A soft answer turneth away wrath: but grievous words stir up anger" (Prov. 15:1). This is like watching the pot so that it will not boil over, making a mess requiring a major cleanup. If we keep joy in our lives, we can sing merrily and pray more easily instead of becoming empty and dry.

Prisms and Rainbows

"Mom, look at that rainbow on the ceiling!" exclaimed five-year-old Austin. "It's so pretty, but how did it get there?"

"Come here, Son. Do you see this glass object that Mrs. Martin gave me hanging in the window? It is called a *prism*, and when the sun shines through it, it creates a rainbow on the floor, walls, and ceiling," explained Mother.

Then she asked him if he remembered the rainbow they had seen in the sky several days before. He answered that he did, and then he asked, "But, Mom, is there a big prism in the sky for the sun to shine through and that's what made the rainbow?"

"No, Son," she answered. Then she went on to explain that a rainbow is caused by the sun shining through a mist or droplets of water.

Mom knew this to be a good time to present a truth to her little son, so she told him if he would live close to God then Jesus could shine in and through him, making his nature beautiful to others, and he would be a reflection of Jesus.

"A new commandment I give unto you, That ye love one another; as I have loved you, that ye also love one another" (John 13:34).

"Then spake Jesus again unto them saying, I am the light of the world: he that followeth me shall not walk in darkness, but shall have the light of life" (John 8:12).

Pride and Juggling

John was asked to have devotions at school. He wanted to tell the children about pride, about how it can only bring harm and disaster into our lives.

First of all, he found three balls that were all the same size but not the same color. Then he found a ball that was larger and prettier than the others. Now he was ready to go to school for devotions.

After the children were through singing, John stepped up to the front with his paper sack. The curiosity of the children was piqued, and they wondered, "What is in that sack?"

Before showing the balls to the children, John talked about pride, how when we are puffed up with it, it will hinder us. Then John took the three balls that were the same size and juggled with them. That was fun to watch and looked so easy and effortless.

As John juggled, he talked some more. He explained, we can work together or be in unison with others if we are small in our own eyes. Next he introduced the large pretty ball to the children. Everyone agreed that it was pretty. So John exchanged the large ball for one of the smaller balls. For a short while, a very short while, he juggled with the two smaller balls and the one larger one. It soon became evident that the large ball was a hindrance. It did not work to have two small balls and one large one. John explained that this is how it is with people who become puffed up, thinking they are better than others. For a short time, it may seem to be fine, but it soon will become evident that there is a problem. Then he read Proverbs 16:18, "Pride goeth before destruction, and an haughty spirit before a fall."

He again exchanged the large ball for a smaller one, and the smoothness of juggling with three uniform balls was fun to watch. It was easy to see the lesson of pride and humility. "Yea, all of you be subject one to another, and be clothed with humility: for God resisteth the proud, and giveth grace to the humble" (1 Peter 5:5).

ABC's of Christian Living

Dear Son,

You met the Lord eight years ago. It has not always been an easy road. Let us look at the alphabet and see if we can discover some words of encouragement.

A   Assurance of salvation. What a blessed assurance when I know I am His and He is mine.

B   Begin each day with God, reading His Word and conversing with Him so you can bear all things.

C   Consecrate your life to God. Jesus gave His life for you, so you should give Him yours.

D   Discipline yourself in all areas of your life; dare to live right.

E   Every day is a chance to live for God.

F   Faith in God is the answer and pleases Him.

G   God's grace always exceeds and pardons our sin.

H   Humble yourself to always be a Christian.

I   "I am determined to serve the Lord" should be your goal.

J   Joy of salvation is your delight.

K   Keep near to the cross.

L   Love and loyalty in service to Christ are a great combination.

M   "More like Jesus" should be a daily prayer.

N   Never alone when Jesus is your friend.

O   Obey the Holy Spirit.

P   Praying and praising go hand in hand.

Q   Quietness with the Lord earns one's strength.

R   "Ready to do His will" should be your motto.

S   Share the sunshine of your life, singing often.

T   Throw out the lifeline to others, and you will gain strength.

U   Under His wings is safety and rest.

V Value your Christian home, parents, brothers, and sisters.

W Walk daily with your Savior.

X Xtol (extol) the love of Christ; tell what He has done for you.

Y Yield not to temptation.

Z Zion is our goal!

Wishing you a successful Christian life,

Mom

Loyal and Faithful

Mittens, a cat, was a much loved family pet. He joined our household when he was a few weeks old. He was treated quite favorably and given certain rights that any cat would enjoy.

When young, he always stayed around the house. After a time, he became more inquisitive and daring, wanting to visit the neighborhood. Ah, it was so interesting. There were so many places to visit, so much to see and do. Home was dear, too, and he did want to be loyal to those who took care of him, so he would always come back.

Then came the day when Mittens did not come home for his supper; in fact, he was gone all night. The children wondered what had happened to him, but they were relieved when he returned in the morning.

This became a way of life for our cat. He would disappear for a night, but he would always come home in the morning. He maybe was not faithful, but he tried to be loyal to his caregivers.

One morning, however, he did not come home. He did not come home all day, nor the next, or next. After Mittens was gone for a week, the children decided he must have been killed.

Six weeks later, early one morning when I was outside, what did I see but Mittens coming down the driveway. He acted like he had never been gone. We wondered at his reappearance but decided we would probably never know where he had been.

About two or three weeks later, we had a garage sale. Mittens was there walking around and being just as curious as any cat can be. When one of the women who was shopping saw Mittens, she exclaimed, "Why, Buttercup, here you are. I always wondered what happened to you!" Then she told me how she had fed him and given him some excellent care.

But Mittens decided he would stay with us. Never again did he go stay with anyone else.

I am thinking about our lives, how the ways of the world can entice us. The devil will tempt us with so many things; there is much to see and do. It seems we try one thing, and another item or two pop up in its place. It is all so interesting; we just have to try it all.

We need to remain loyal and faithful to God to win a crown of life.

Covetousness

The Purple Martins were traveling northward. As they traveled, they chatted among themselves. Mrs. Martin said she was weary of traveling and would be glad to settle down in her summer apartment. Mr. Martin said he was looking forward to a tasty meal of flies and beetles. He went on to say he was glad their summer home was in the southern part of America where winged insects were plentiful.

At long last they arrived at their destination. They planned to live in the apartment they had lived in the last several years, so they flew with confidence to their dwelling. Before going in, Mrs. Martin sat on the railing of the porch and sang her thanks and praises for being back home. She was startled and indignant when she felt a breeze and a brush of wings against her beak. The next thing she knew was that someone was in her apartment! Surely it was Mr. Martin, but that was unlikely as he was on a scouting expedition, and he was always faithful in his duties. Then a thought hit her, "Was it Mrs. Sparrow?"

Mrs. Martin hopped to the doorway. Sure enough, it was Mrs. Sparrow. Why of all things! The nerve! Mrs. Martin screamed at Mrs. Sparrow, "What do you think you're doing here? This is my apartment and has been for years."

"I moved in last winter when it was empty, plus I really like the view. So I've started building my nest," explained Mrs. Sparrow. "Besides that, I've wanted this place for a long time, and I just decided to take it."

"Never mind that," replied Mrs. Martin. "You will have to go, and if I have to evict you myself." With that Mrs. Martin pecked Mrs. Sparrow unmercifully on her head.

Paws, the cat on the farm, came running when he heard the birds fighting. He knew if he would wait, he might get a tasty bird. Before long, dust and feathers were flying, and Paws was watching. All of a sudden, he made a leap, grabbed a falling bird, Mrs. Sparrow, and ran.

Peace and quiet reigned. Mrs. Martin bustled about getting her house ready for a family. If she could give you a word of advice, she would say, "Don't covet or want what is not yours. It is wrong to try to get someone else's possessions, and it can bring you grief."

"Thou shalt not covet..." (Exod. 20:17).

Homemaking

I have been watching a scene of homemaking.

Mr. and Mrs. Swallow flew in from the distant south. They chose to build their nest in a corner above a light on our covered patio. That was a good spot for me, too. Now I could watch their every move from the window above my work space.

They worked together with unity and goodwill, agreeing on how large to build their nest and what to build it with. Never once did I hear them argue or bicker with one another. I did hear them chatting together, but it appeared they were conversations of goodwill and peace.

When the nest was built, they took time to line it with grass and feathers. They wanted it just right, cozy and warm. I knew they were preparing for someone special.

One day soon after their careful nest building, I saw Mrs. Swallow sitting patiently on the nest. Mr. Swallow sat close by on the blade of the ceiling fan in quiet devotion. He was sitting close enough to watch and be of assistance or to chat with his mate. Sometimes he would fly away and come back with a morsel of food for the Mrs. Occasionally, I would see Mrs. Swallow leave the nest for some exercise; she would go to a nearby fishpond for a drink and splash. Oftentimes, Mr. Swallow would fly to the nest, sitting there until his mate returned.

At last I saw Mrs. Swallow fly off and return with food in her beak. That is when I saw Sonny, Missy, and Tootsie for the first time. They popped their little heads up, begging for food. Now Papa and Mama are kept very busy. When the weather is stormy, Mama sits on top of the nest, giving comfort and shielding the young from the storm. Sometimes Mama sits on the edge of the nest and Papa sits close by, a lovely picture of contentment and satisfaction. Once I saw Mama leave the nest, joining Papa for some rest on his favorite perch, the ceiling fan.

Is not this a beautiful picture of home? Your parents want to work together in charity and harmony and prepare a safe place for you. They have a common goal in mind, a haven of love and contentment for you. That is a bit of Heaven on earth!

Little Is Much

"Mother," called Jacob, "where are you?"

"Here, son, on the back porch," answered Mother. "I am baking some fish and barley bread for our supper."

"Daniel just came by and told me that Jesus is going to be in the desert near Bethsaida tomorrow. May I go listen to Jesus with Daniel?"

"If you bring in three jars of water before you go and the rest of your chores are done before you leave, then you may go," Mother said.

"Oh, good," cried Jacob. "I'll even go to bed earlier tonight so I can get up earlier."

The next morning Mother was not surprised to see Jacob up early doing his chores. She decided to make some extra barley loaves and bake some more fish so she could send a lunch with him.

Finally, Jacob was on his way, and what a beautiful morning it was. Oh, the thrill of looking forward to listening to Jesus! Jacob had heard Him speak once before, and it was so interesting.

As Jacob was hurrying along, he saw Daniel ahead of him and yelled, "Wait for me. Let's go together." In no time, they saw a group of people and knew they had come to the right place. They were soon enthralled by Jesus and His sermon. Hours passed, but Jacob did not remember he had brought lunch with him.

Toward evening Jacob felt a tap on his shoulder and turned to look. A kindly looking man asked him if he had brought his lunch in the basket he was hanging on to. Jacob glanced down and realized he still had his lunch basket clasped in his hand. Why, he had forgotten all about his lunch! Then the man asked him if he would share his lunch with Jesus. Jacob's stomach growled. But, yes, he would share.

Jacob thrust his lunch basket into Andrew's hand and said, "I'll give it all to Him."

"Thanks, young lad," Andrew said and hurried over to Jesus.

Jacob watched intently, and what he saw astonished him. Jesus looked up into heaven and said, "Thank You, Father in heaven, for this food." Jacob was amazed to see Jesus handing all twelve of his helpers food from his basket. His amazement increased as he saw the helpers give food to everyone! How thankful he was that he had brought lunch with him and that he had given it to Jesus. He could not wait to tell Mother that Jesus blessed the lunch she gave him and that it had fed so many people. How astonished she would be!

This shows us that when we give our all, no matter how small, Jesus can bless it, and it can be a blessing to others (Luke 9:10-17).

Flying High and Safe

A minister and his wife were watching this scene not long ago. It was a scene that held much meaning to them, as it is so true to life.

A father and mother bird were trying to teach their young to fly. The young bird perched on the edge of the nest. He appreciated his home; it was so safe and secure. Nevertheless, the call of nature wooed him to leave his home. So Mother and Father stayed close by, willing to help when needed.

Before long, the young bird teetered and fell to the ground. Now he had some new scenery. It was a whole new experience. There were so many new things to see and do. In no time, he forgot the need to learn to fly. He did not realize there were dangers around, that it may not be safe for a young bird to be on the ground. He did not realize there was a menacing, stalking cat that wanted to snatch him, to have him for a good meal.

But Father and Mother knew the dangers. They tried to convince him to fly, to flutter his wings. But Junior was having so much fun. There was no rush as far as he was concerned. Soon other birds came to join the anxious parents. There was an urgent need; the young one was not safe.

Then the cat came around the corner of the house, and how anxious all the birds became. Such a loud chattering and urging, a pleading for Junior to apply himself to his great need of getting off the ground. One of the older birds went to the young one and took his wing and pushed him, telling him he just had to fly. The birds stayed with Junior till their own lives were in danger, then they had to flee for their own safety. In no time, the cat pounced and had the tender young bird in his grasp, and the young bird's life was snuffed out.

Young friend, when parents or the minister urge you to a higher standard of living, know this that they only have love and care for you. They can see and understand the wiles of the evil one and want to help you fly to new heights in Christ Jesus. Should it become necessary, they are willing to give their all to rescue you from the evil one's grasp.

"...he which converteth the sinner from the error of his way shall save a soul from death..." (James 5:20).

Going Home to Heaven

Chuck, a nine-year-old lad, had a beloved companion in his golden retriever, Duke. What wonderful times they had going fishing and hunting together. It was a joy just to be with each other. Dad would even let Duke ride in the back of the pick-up when they needed to run to town on an errand. Mom, though, was something else. She never allowed Duke to enter the house.

A year before on Chuck's birthday, he had received a small tent for a birthday gift. What delight when Dad helped him put it up in their woods so he and Chuck could spend a night there. Chuck's pleasure knew no bounds when he realized Duke would be able to join the camp out. Duke was ecstatic to be in on the adventure; his tail did not quit wagging. It became a common occurrence for Chuck and Duke to spend a night in the woods together.

Several months after Chuck's ninth birthday, he went for a bike ride with Duke trailing behind. Of course, occasionally Duke would run ahead, but he would stop and wait for Chuck, seeming to say, "Hurry along, Champ. There is lots to see."

They went along merrily until there was a squeal of tires. No one knew how it happened, but Chuck was hit by a car and thrown from his bike. Duke saw Chuck lying on the road. Duke went to Chuck and whined, but he received no answer.

Back home, Dad knew something was wrong when Duke dashed up to him and whined urgently. Duke ran off and looked back , waiting for Dad. Dad followed Duke to where Chuck lay. Chuck was carried home and laid on the couch in the living room. Several hours later he regained consciousness. When he awakened, Mother and Dad were right there—and Duke was there, too! Then Dad told Chuck that the angels would soon come and take him home to Heaven.

"What is Heaven like?" Chuck asked.

Mom told him that Heaven was a wonderful place and that he would be with Jesus there. She told Chuck how happy Duke was to be in the house, because Chuck was there. Duke would come up to Chuck, glad to be with him. Then Duke would walk around the room, exploring this place he had never been before. Always he would come back to Chuck, wanting to be with him.

Mom told Chuck that this is how it would be when he got to Heaven. First, he would meet Jesus who died for him so he could go there. Then he would tour Heaven and see treasures he had never seen before, but he would always come back to Jesus—he would not want to be away from Jesus very long; he would want to be with Jesus because he would love Jesus so much.

Mom went on to tell Chuck that it would not be long till she and Dad would join him in Heaven, and they would never be parted again. There was a smile on Chuck's face and his hand was resting on Duke's head when the angels came and took him to Heaven.

Poetry

My Daily Prayer

Oh, Lord, I know you see my plans, my ambitions, and my dreams
You know about my worries, my fears, and all my doubts;
You feel my hurts, my disappointments and my many frustrations
All my wants, my wishes and desires, can you help me work them out?

I need you, Lord, to take my plans and somehow make them yours.
Take my dreams and ambitions, too, I want them in your will.
Lord, take away the doubts and fears, then in their place send faith
To calm the waves of worry when you whisper, 'Peace, be still.'

Then come the hurts, the disappointments, they can really get me down
Till I realize once again, Lord, that you really understand.
Just carry me through the cloudy times till the sun shines through again
Then help me, Lord, to ever hold to your unchanging hand.

My wants, my wishes and my desires need your guiding hand of love
To keep the right perspective, Lord, to keep my goal in view.
When the trials come and the way seems hard, it's then that I remember
I only have to lean on you and know you'll see me through.

Thank you, Lord, for loved ones and my friends and dear family.
They help me through the many valleys with just a word or two.
Each day I count my many blessings that you have given me
And with your help, Lord, let me be . . . a shining light for you.

The Lighthouse

There's a lighthouse – a beacon light on the dark seas
It's guiding the boat – my boat – pointing the way.
With faith and trust in its guiding light, I let it lead me
into the deep waters, away from the rocky shores of confusion,
and from the shallow waters of doubts and fears
that come along the way.
The clouds will come, the rains will fall, and the winds will blow
But if I keep my eyes on that guiding light,
that beacon on the dark sea,
I need not fear what lies ahead.

For that light will be true and forever there to see me through
each trial, each heartache, each lonely hour
and guide me on to that final rest – my Eternal home.

Thank you, Lord, for being my Guiding Light, my Lighthouse, a shining
beacon light on the sea of life.

Faith and Trust

A pilot flies his big airplane on clear and cloudy days.

When the sky is clear and cloudless, and the sun sends forth its rays,

He puts his faith and trust in gauges and the message they portray.

But when the sky gets rather hazy and the clouds chase the sun away,

There's a rule that he must follow and his faith and trust must stay

Upon the gauges on that panel, they'll not let him go astray.

If he keeps his eyes just focused, trust will keep his plane aright

When his feelings tell him strongly that he's in an awful plight.

He thinks his plane is headed any way but what is right.

He knows from past experience that his gauges surely tell,

Exactly which way he is going and he knows that all is well.

Let's take a look, dear traveler, as we journey on our way,

When the path that we are walking is filled with blessings every day,

We put our faith and trust in Jesus and to Him we daily pray.

But when the path gets rough and rocky and the sun is hid from view

There's a promise God has given and to that promise He'll be true.

He'll not leave us nor forsake us, he will surely see us through.

If we keep our eyes just focused, trust will keep us going right.

But when dark doubts and fears crowd 'round us and we cannot see the light

We sometimes wonder which way to turn and there is an awful fright.

But if we can from past experience draw the strength that we do need

From the One that won't forsake us let Him be the one to lead

And we keep our eyes just focused, we'll be free, yes, free indeed.

If we have that faith in good times that is grounded on the truth

When tests and trials come our way and dark clouds are blowing through

Underneath the stormy surface is a faith that keeps us true.

A Dozen Red Roses

Written with love and my blessings to you,

Love,

Mom

A dozen red roses all covered with dew
And given to portray my wishes for you.

One rose for the love you are sharing today
May it continue to grow and be a way
Of bluer skies and colors of brighter hue
As you walk life's pathway, it will see you through.

One rose for peace, and it comes from both knowing
That this is God's will, your life you'll be sharing.
Always hold on to that God given blessing
Be true to each other, never quit loving.

A rose for the joy that will come in giving
Yourselves to each other. Sharing and caring
And in sickness or health, whether rich or poor
Let him know he's loved when he walks in the door.

One rose for happiness . . . I hope that you will
Pray each day for His blessings, and then be still,
Put your hands in His, let Him lead and guide
True happiness comes when in Him you abide.

A rose for God's grace . . . grace enough in your life
To weather the storms as a husband and wife.
When the stormy winds blow, and surely they will,
"I'm sorry, forgive me" their place they will fill.

One rose for a caring heart. One that reaches out
To others around who hit storms all about,
And be willing to lend a helping hand, too,
When there is a need and small things you can do.

A rose for a happy home. A mansion fair
Or a little cottage, a small garden there,
Let the door be opened with love as the key
For stranger or friend or your dear family.

A rose for patience. Patience as you both learn
To give or to take as from two lives you yearn
To become one in heart, in soul and in mind
With the Lord's will and yours forever entwined.

One rose for friends. For friends make life beautiful
When heartaches and woes come your way they help pull
You out of the deep shadows of grief and pain
Help you see that there will be sunshine again.

A rose in mem'ry of your Dad who has gone
Before us to lead us, with God, not alone.
Remember the blessings that he did bestow
On you, my dear children, before he did go.

And then a rose for an ever thankful heart
For all the blessings and love He doth impart.
A thankful heart is a contented heart, too
Today my prayer, "May God richly bless you."

The last of the dozen is last, but not least.
The one rose for Heaven, where we will meet
Our loved ones so dear, who have gone on before.
Let's all strive to see them on Heaven's bright shore.

Always remember that the prayers you pray,
Will open the doors of Heav'n along the way.
And from this day forward, until death do part,
Just cherish the love that God put in you heart.

Index